AF479391

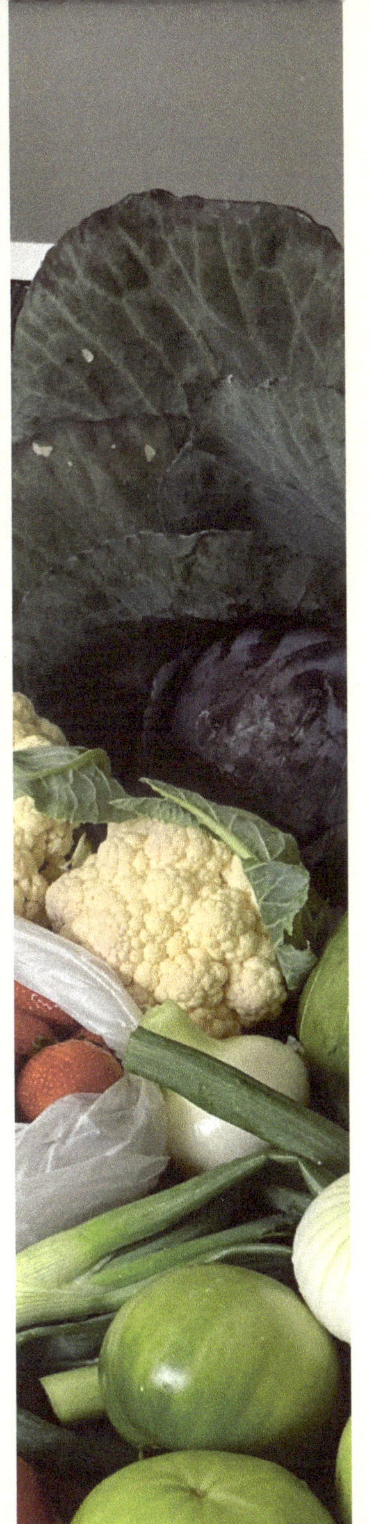

Faith, Food & Art:

Surviving the Pandemics of 2020
A Visual Journal of Arts-Based Self-Care

A "tiny book" in the series, How Did I Get Here? My Life: Stories & Wisdom

To the multitudes gathered on the hill, spiritually, financially, emotionally and physically hungry, sick and wanting, God says,

"Tell everyone to sit down."
(based on John 6:1-10)

INTRODUCTION
I was determined not to let this virus kill me!

This tiny book tells a part of my story during the COVID-19 quarantine. Mostly a picture book, it documents many of my creative works made during one of the most challenging years for the world. In April, Disney (where I worked part-time for fun) closed, as did my church. So I mindfully and intentionally increased my creative and meditative time as a way of thriving and healing during the COVID-19, toxic political & racial injustice pandemics of 2020. Artmaking and spiritual study became two of the major pieces of my self-care plan. The creations themselves stand as products, in some cases, of my God-given talents, and in other cases, as newly acquired skills, insights and opportunities for mastery.   They reflect my groanings & prayers, as well as my assurance of God's Light and Hope. More, the creations presented opportunities to express the fruits of my faith through sharing the food with neighbors and as holiday gifts; creating cards with which to stay connected to friends & family, and through spreading joy and showing kindness, generosity and love to others.

I intended the book, itself a creative work of many hours, to also share and communicate the joy I experienced while creating, as well as to convey the integrative nature of creativity and faith. The brief commentaries accompanying the images shed light not only on descriptive features, but also on these integrative dimensions. Throughout the book I also highlight nine (9) major elements of an effective self-care plan.

I share the book with you in the hope that it nourishes your spirit and sense of beauty as well as encourages your engagement in creativity and holistic, arts-based, faith-centered self-care.

If you would like some guidance in formulating your own self-care journey or plan, you can leave a comment/request on my blog/website below.

Vivian Nix-Early, Ph.D., MTBC. Psychologist, creative arts therapist, educator, consultant. Read and see more at www.viviannixearly.life

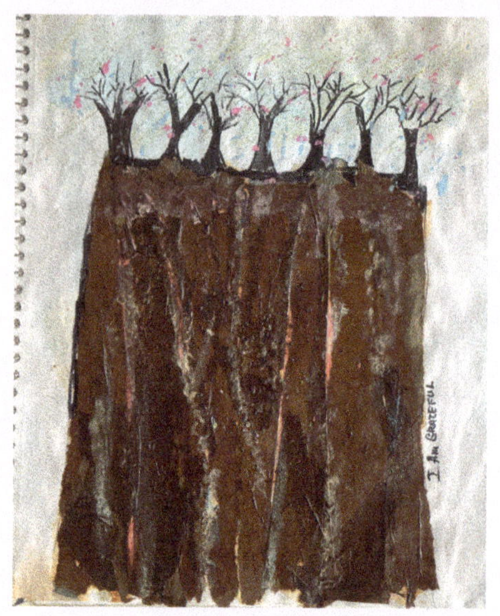

"Deep Roots - I am Grateful"
Mediums: Watercolor, tissue paper, marker, glitter
By Vivian Nix-Early

ACKNOWLEDGMENTS

I am grateful for my parents, Big Mom, Grandmothers & extended family who believed that to be full citizens of the world you must practice faith and be involved in the arts. And, they were all great cooks!

I am grateful for my business partner and best friend, Dr. J. Nathan Corbitt who has, for 20+ years, influenced my perspectives on art and faith as critical components for actively and practically serving the most vulnerable people in the world.

I am also grateful for my former student Ann, who, before grocery stores ramped up their delivery & drive-up options, made sure I had everything I needed.

Sabbathing is like making a good cup of tea!

Two months into the quarantine, I developed the habit of illustrating spiritual messages that I wanted to plant in my memory. The power of visual art is its ability to create symbols that can represent a series of complex concepts more efficiently than words. After listening to a sermon by Student Ministries Director Anthony Maccagnano (First United Methodist Church, Clermont, FL), I made these sketches of glasses of tea. He used the metaphor of making tea to give an encouraging message about the importance of sabbathing and resting as a part of seeing things change.

Like this steeping tea bag, Sabbathing* often requires quiet waiting and watching for both internal and external transformation, listening and direction. The steeping process, which results in more depth of flavor, robust color and aroma, can then lead to more power and action.

I realized from this quarantine period that I was not really allowing myself to become the steeping tea bag. I've been dipping the bag in and out a few times here and there, moving too quickly and feeling weaker and less powerful against the onslaught of racial and political injustice, isolation, grief and health trauma.

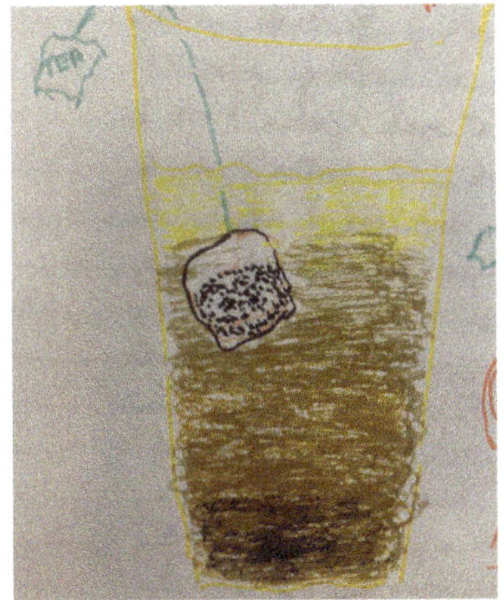

FAITH

The pandemics of 2020 gave me the opportunity to sit down from all of my busyness, stress and worry to consider how I should be spending my time if I and the world are to be healed.

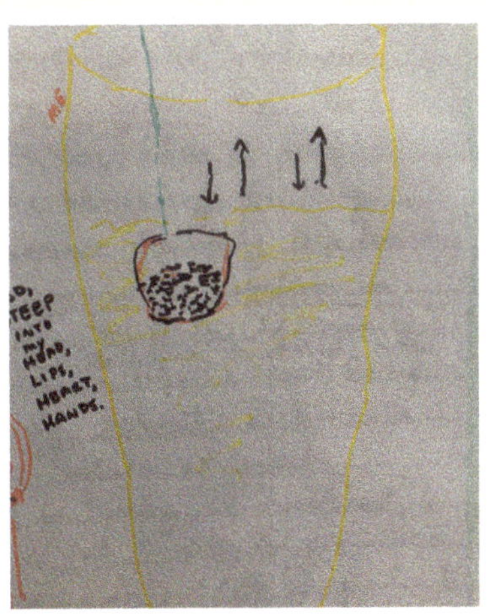

*Sabbathing: a verb understood by me to mean ceasing or stopping; stepping out of the chaos of the world into the consideration of God's promises in order to more effectively partner with Him in acts of love & justice. It is a change of focus, not circumstance.

Self-care element: Positive mantras, often connected with faith, bolster a hopeful attitude and perspective. One of mine became "Transformation requires Steeping". I repeat it when patience and listening are required.

FOOD

For the last 15 years, I've been moving ever closer to eating a healthier, more plant-based diet. At 71 years of age, I welcomed the opportunity to dive into discovering and creating beautiful food that is at the same time good for the mind and body.

For the most part, I have not created the recipes depicted in this book - plenty of people have done that. The joy has come in taking what's on a page and artfully creating a 3D version of the printed words, adding my own creative touches here and there, often changing ingredients and methods, and sometimes inventing my own recipes, like the two originals on this page.

Self-care element: A healthy diet fuels our brain and boosts our immune system.

I created this layered power-foods breakfast sandwich with a piece of my homemade whole grain rustic bread. Toast the bread, drizzle with olive oil and rub with a whole garlic clove. Layer smoked cooked salmon & avocado. Sprinkle with lemon juice, crushed red pepper & sea salt. Top with hard-boiled egg slices.

Health Note: The Omega-3 fatty acids, healthy fats, antioxidants, vitamins, minerals, fiber, protein & carotenoids in these ingredients reduce inflammation & help maintain healthy skin, eye, cardiovascular, digestive and brain health.

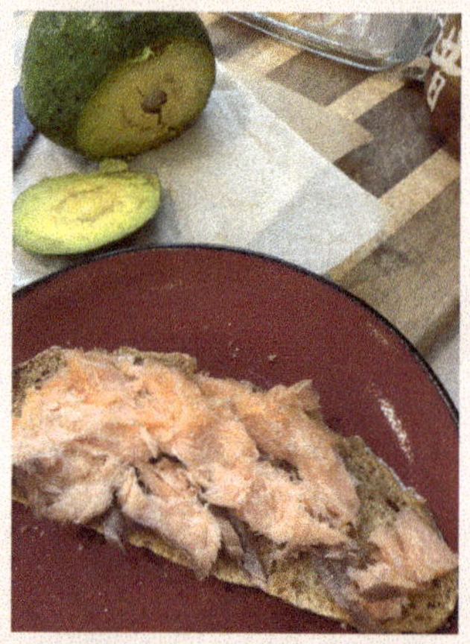
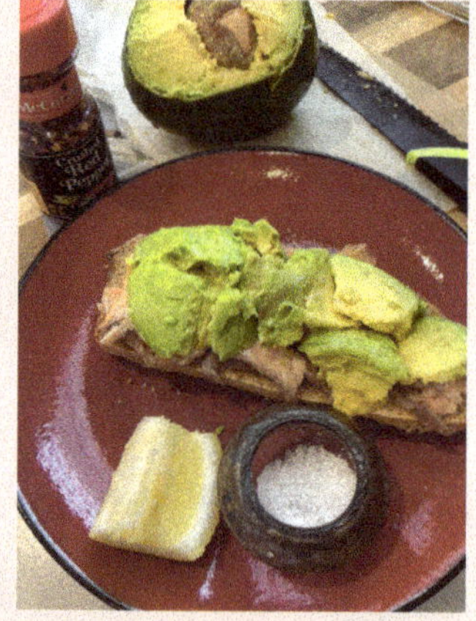
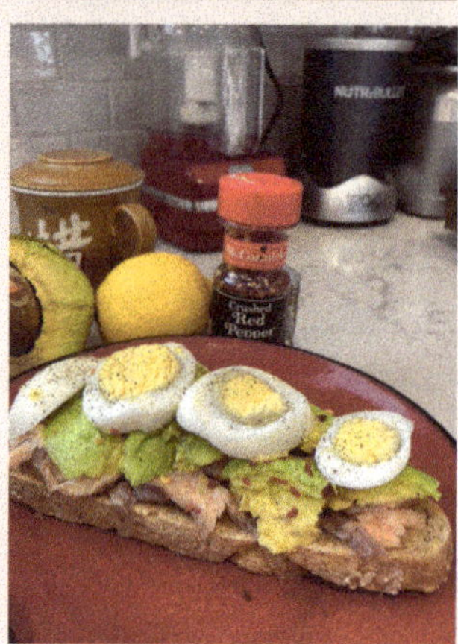
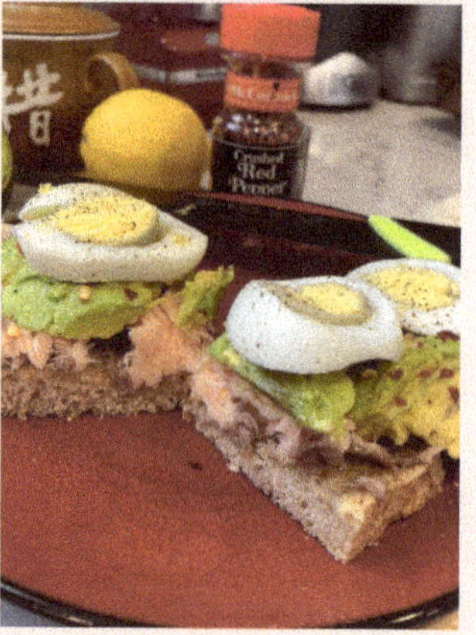

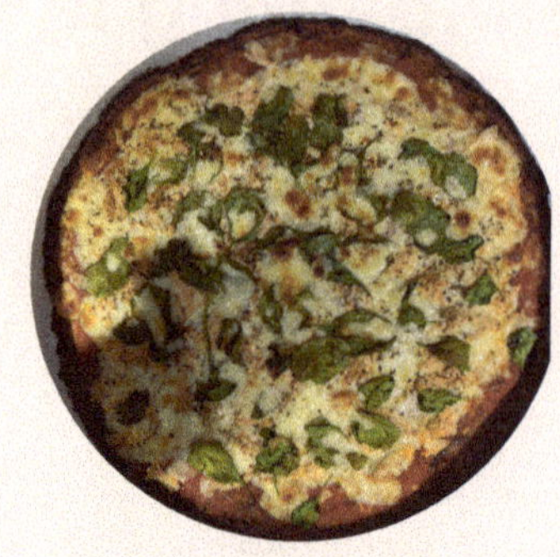
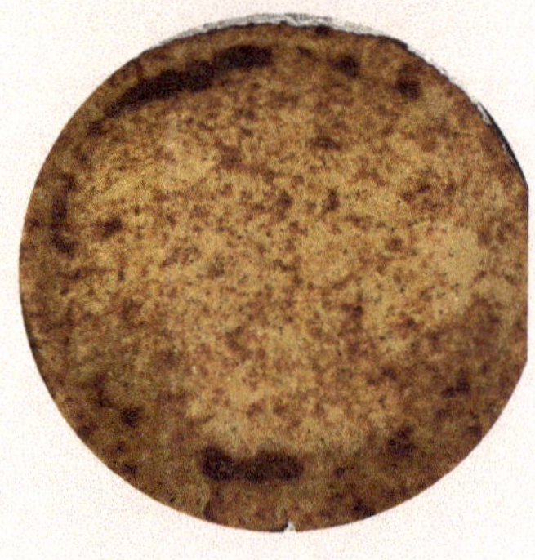

I started this cauliflower crust pizza by ricing one head of cauliflower in a food processor and using any good online recipe for the crust. Get creative with your toppings. I used tomato sauce, shredded chicken, mozzarella, spinach, oregano & basil.

Health Note. Try making your own cauliflower crust pizza. It's a healthier alternative to regular crust: lower in calories & carbs; high in vitamin K & C, fiber, antioxidants; gluten free, strengthens immunity & lowers blood pressure.

ART

We are made in the likeness of our Creator. When we create, we are expressing a part of our God-image.

Artmaking is adult play. It is therapeutic. Creativity is innately healing. It is the opposite of helplessness. The process of artmaking teaches us how to heal and mend, and presents many metaphors for living well. It helps us create new rituals and traditions that order and integrate our lives, and reveals new purpose & meaning. The process gives us new skills, affirmation, and facilitates resilience. Fabric, visual and craft art works in this book are all original works by me. All of the food images are my creations, but many were made using recipes published by others.

Self-care element: Creative experiences and activities (including the arts, music, movement, journaling, and creative writing) help us transcend the chaos of the moment, increase healthy brain chemistry and neuronal activity, help us deepen and express inner emotions, offer a sense of mastery, and provide nourishment for the soul and spirit.

TO MY DAD

In a moment of mortality,
You said you weren't the Dad you wanted to be.
Your time was spent in hours working
And scarce resources meant that tangible things didn't abound.
So this letter assures you that what was precious
Is not measured in hours or coins.
Just as you carried this violin around in its velvet case, you carried me around in your
Cashmere heart.
The mellow, melancholy sound of bow across strings reminds me of your compassion for all of us.
Our sweet duets showed me of your Care.
Your melodies led me to value faith, art & justice.
The violin is battered now & resting silent;
But remains a symbol of all the gifts of the Spirit you left to me.

As part of an online art class, we were asked to choose an object in our house that had great meaning, and to detail the story behind it. I sketched this picture of my dad's violin & wrote this "found-art" poem about my dad, Andrew W. Nix, Jr., who died in 2011 on his 88th birthday.

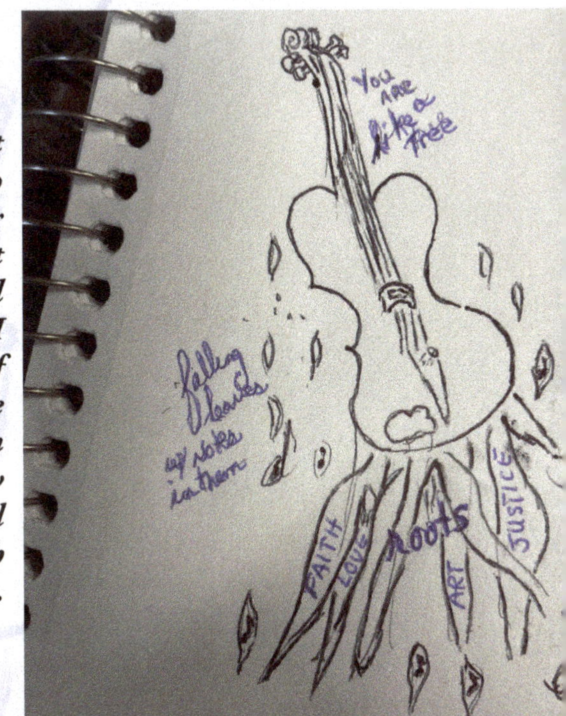

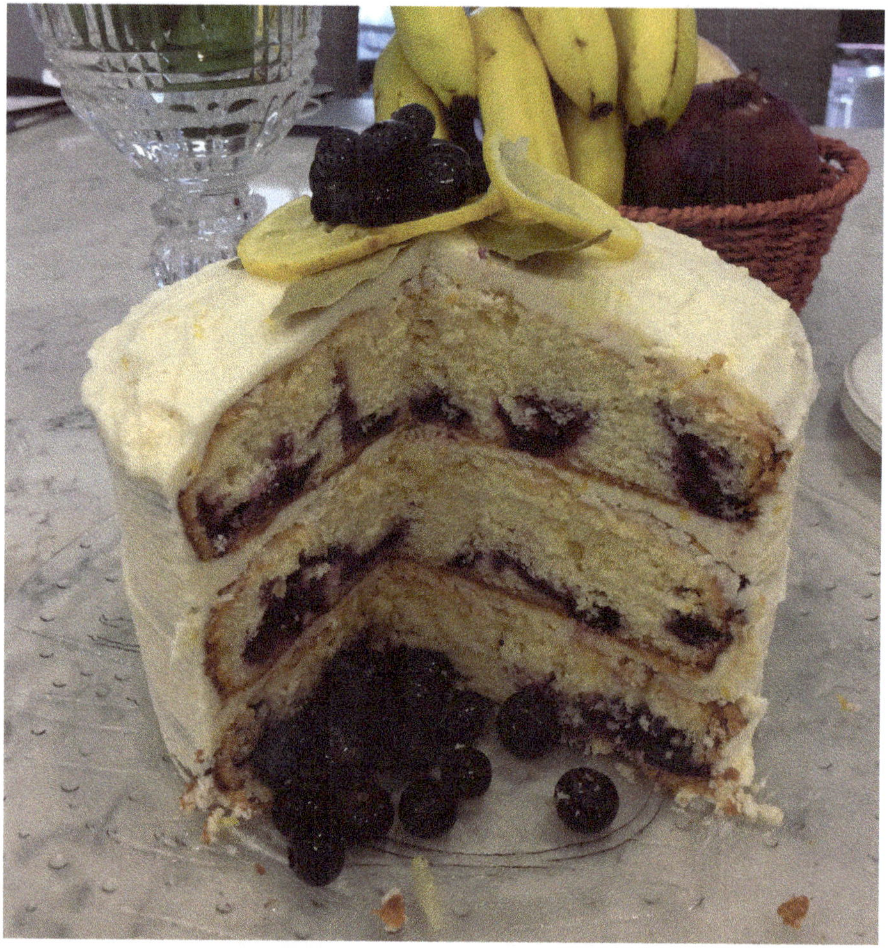

The Corona virus stay-at-home period coincided with one of the fun things I enjoy most in my part of Florida - fruit u-pick seasons: blueberries, strawberries, and my favorite - peach season. During the early days of the pandemic, when the world outside my house felt fearfully unsafe, picking berries & peaches at local farms afforded me the rare chance to "play" outdoors safely. It sparked a weekly baking ritual and gave me an opportunity to share the goods with neighbors. Pictures: Lemon Blueberry Cake, Peach-Ginger Upside Down Cake. The Honey-Sweetened Spiced Peach Jam was an extra treat!

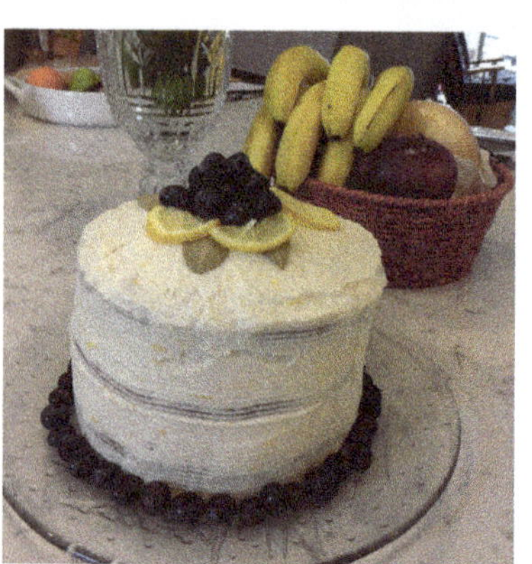

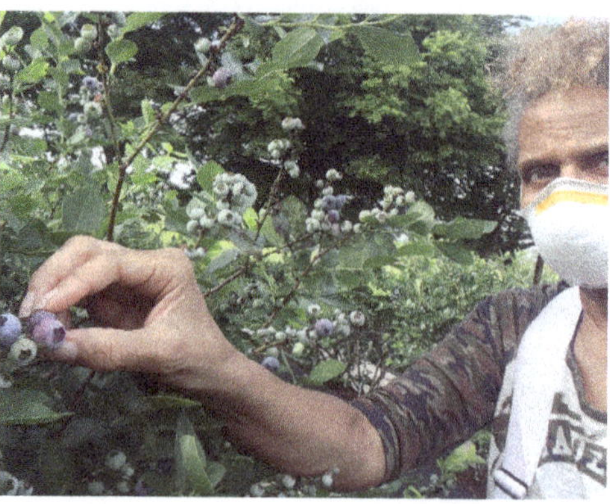

Picking berries at Susie Q's Organic Blues Berry Farm near my home in Groveland, FL.

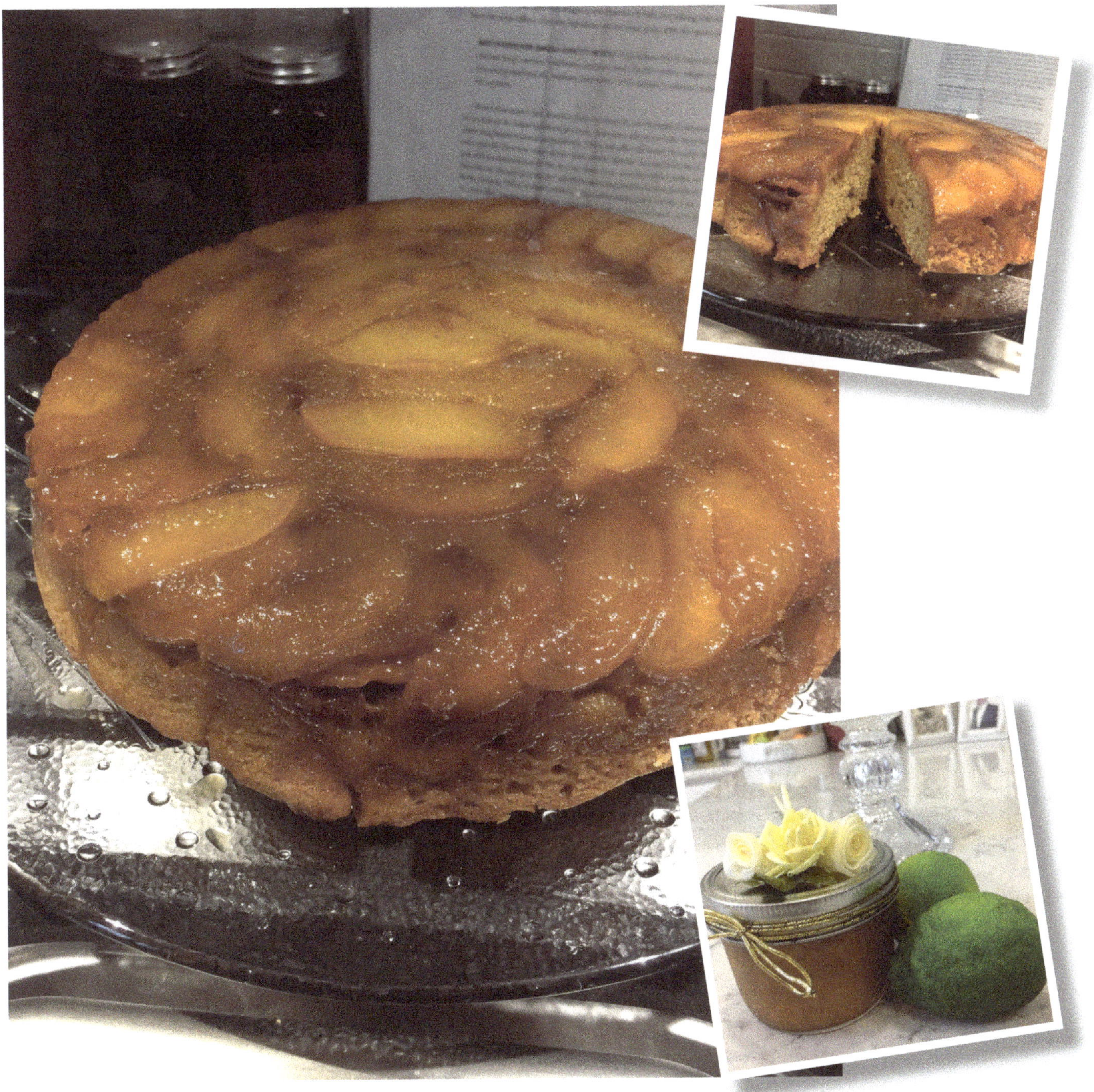

 served by themselves or with avocado toast, became and continue to be a part of my morning ritual and an important part of my self-care plan to engage in healthier eating. I saved a few peaches - with the skin on and sliced - to freeze for making smoothies. One of my favorite energizing smoothies is "Peach Almond Smoothie in a Bowl" (or glass, below). I found it more fun to eat this one than to drink its thick smooth texture. The recipe (opp. pg.) was inspired by one in the Blue Zones Kitchen book, but I've given it a gritty, crunchie, slightly sweeter twist with the addition of honey, unsalted almonds and some homemade snack granola*. Ingredients for some of my favorite original smoothie blends, two of which are pictured here, are included on a subsequent page.

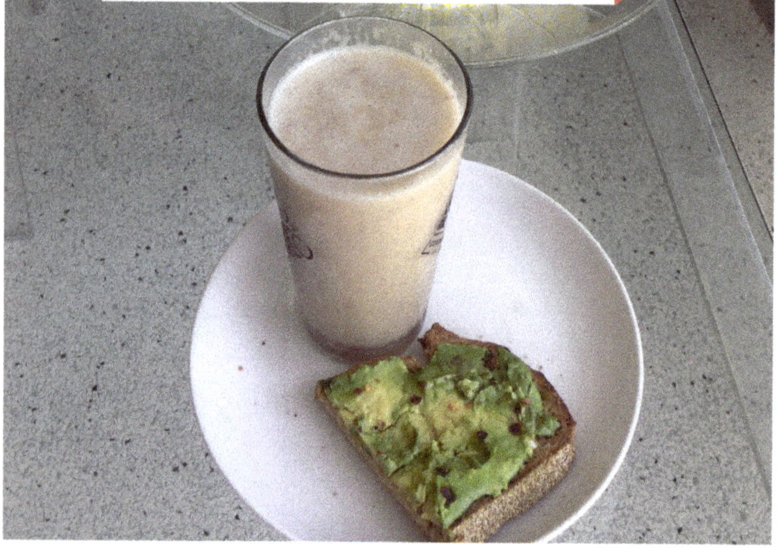

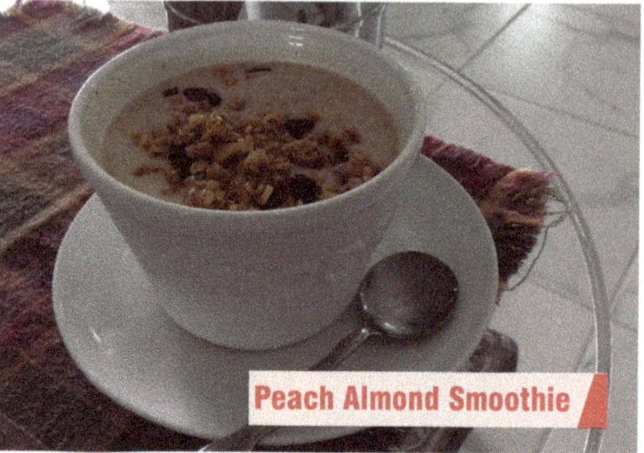

Peach Almond Smoothie

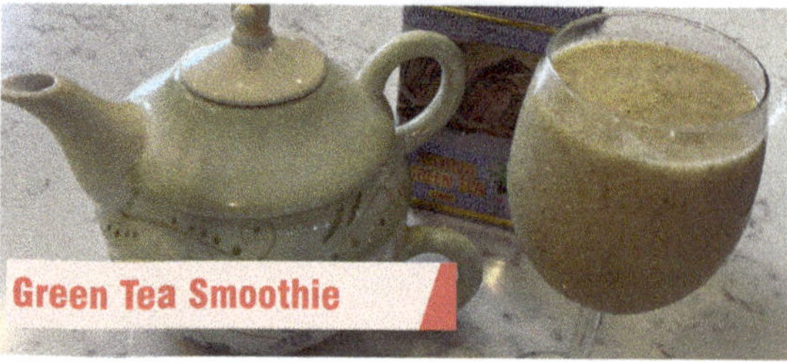

Green Tea Smoothie

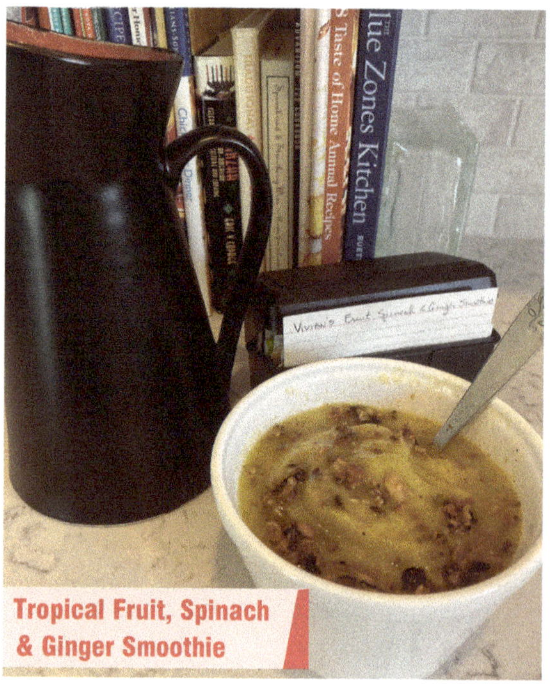

Tropical Fruit, Spinach & Ginger Smoothie

PEACH ALMOND SMOOTHIE IN A BOWL

Ingredients:
3/4 - 1 cup frozen peaches
1 ripe banana
5 oz non-dairy vanilla yoghurt. (I use dairy-free soy yoghurt)
1/2 - 3/4 cup dairy-free milk. (I use oak milk or almond milk and love them both.)
1 tbsp chia or flax seeds
1 tsp (or more, to taste) honey
1 handful of whole, unsalted almonds
1-2 dashes of cayenne pepper
Ice chips

Puree all the ingredients in a blender, adding more ice as needed to create a thick, frosty texture. Pour into a chilled bowl, add granola* on top and enjoy while listening to your favorite relaxing music or watching/listening to the morning sounds of nature.

*Homemade Granola Topping: I make my own granola using oats, raisins, dried cherries, dried cranberries, sunflower seeds, chopped pecans, walnuts pieces, whole raw almonds, wheat germ, honey, maple syrup, corn oil, cinnamon and vanilla. Stir together the oats, oil, honey and syrup. Spread onto a parchment-lined baking sheet and bake in a 375° oven for 20-30 minutes. Stir often, watching carefully to make sure the oats don't burn. Mix together the remaining ingredients and mix into the oats. Bake for 5 more minutes.

Health Note: The capsaicin in cayenne pepper makes it a great addition to a heart-healthy diet. It is a vasodilator, improving blood flow, expanding blood vessels, and thus, reducing blood-pressure. Flax, chia & other seeds are high in omega-3 fatty acids, a good source of fiber & protein, and foster digestion and energy. Bananas, dark chocolate, nuts, coffee, water, oats, yoghurt, avocado and leafy greens are considered high energy-boosting foods. Ginger root boasts a myriad of physical & mental health benefits, and is one of the healthiest things to add to your diet.

MY FAVORITE BLENDS

TROPICAL FRUIT, SPINACH & GINGER SMOOTHIE

Note: Proportions are approximate and can be modified according to taste and the capacity of your blending appliance

Ingredients:

1.5 - 2 cups frozen cut-up fruit: banana, mango, pineapple

Handful of organic baby spinach

1 c. Ginger-honey syrup*

1 c Ginger Kombucha (great probiotics)

1 c Carbonated water (I make my own with a

SodaStream machine)

TROPICAL 3-G SMOOTHIE (GREEN, GRAIN & GINGER)

Ingredients : Frozen pineapple, banana, mango, avocado; kale, cinnamon-vanilla yoghurt, cayenne, uncooked oats, flax seed, ginger syrup, ginger kombucha, water.

BANANA, COFFEE, PEANUT BUTTER SMOOTHIE.

This is my go-to smoothie any day of the week!

Ingredients: Blend 1 banana, a large scoop of peanut or other nut butter, oats, coffee (slightly sweetened), oat or almond milk, cinnamon, dash of unsweetened 100% cacao, flax seed, whole almonds, ice chips.

MANGO, MINT, GREEN TEA SMOOTHIE.

Ingredients: Frozen mango, frozen banana, fresh mint leaves, chia or flax seed, oats, green tea sweetened to taste with honey, ice chips.

*I make this by boiling several large pieces of fresh, peeled organic ginger root in a quart of water and adding honey to taste. I store it in a glass bottle in the refrigerator to have on hand.

At the height of the Black Lives Matter movement in June, I decided to sign up for some online visual art classes, though I possess little drawing skill. Pictures express feelings better than words.

I breathed with the drawing of every line - breathing for George Floyd and for all those who can't because of injustice.

Self-care element: Taking several mindfulness and deep breathing breaks during the day & during creative activity promotes awareness of how we are feeling and "being present" in the moment. They help us listen & restore.

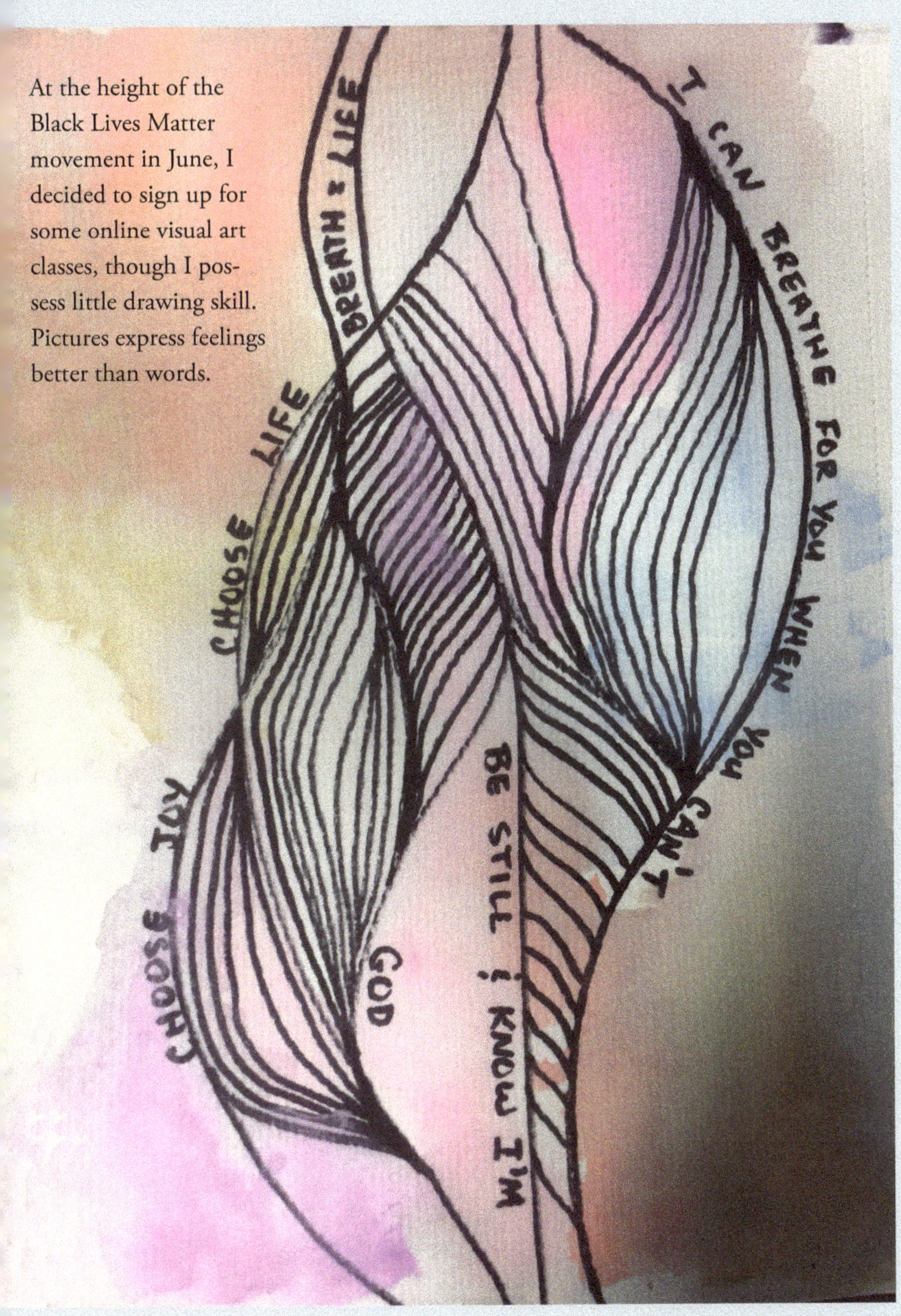

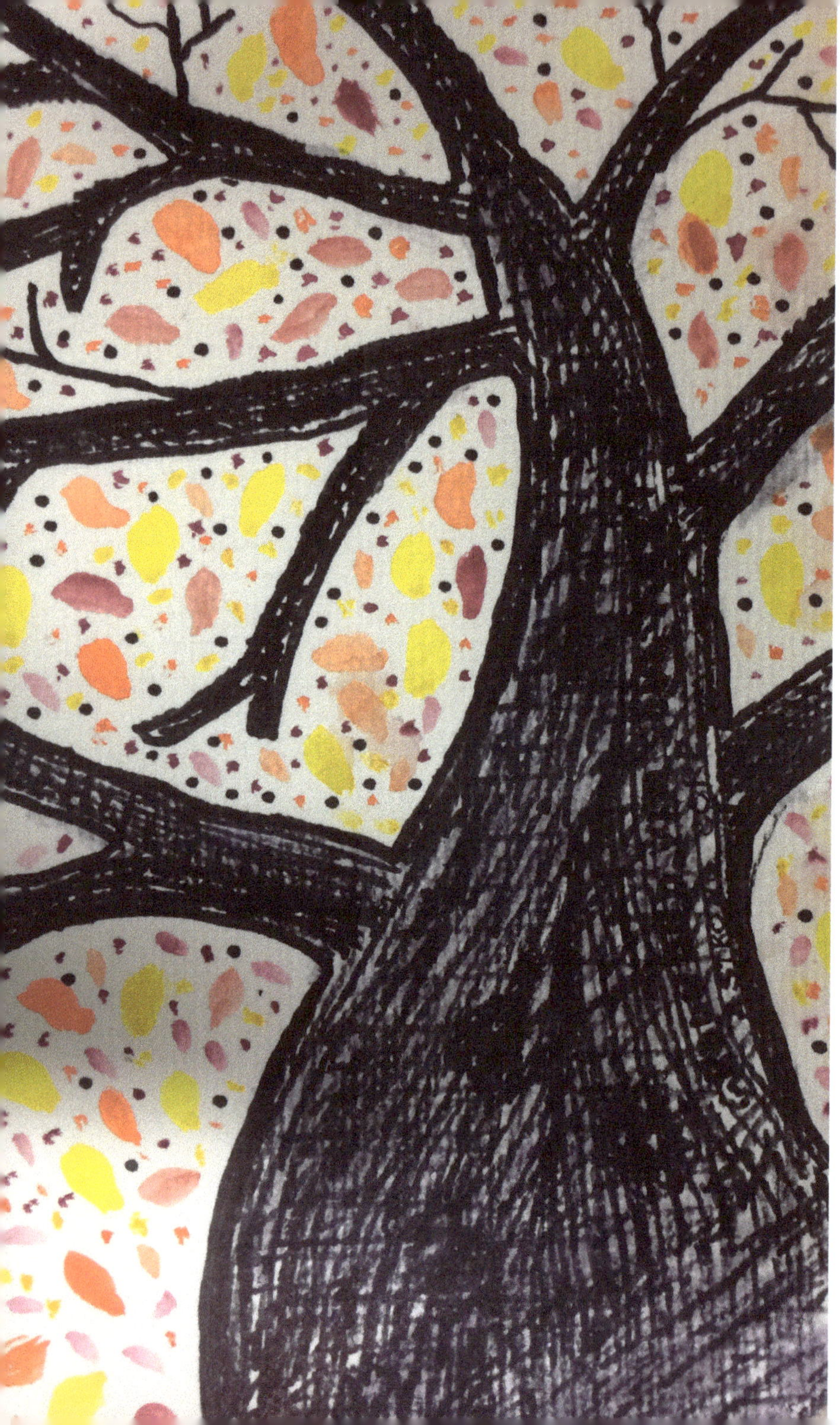

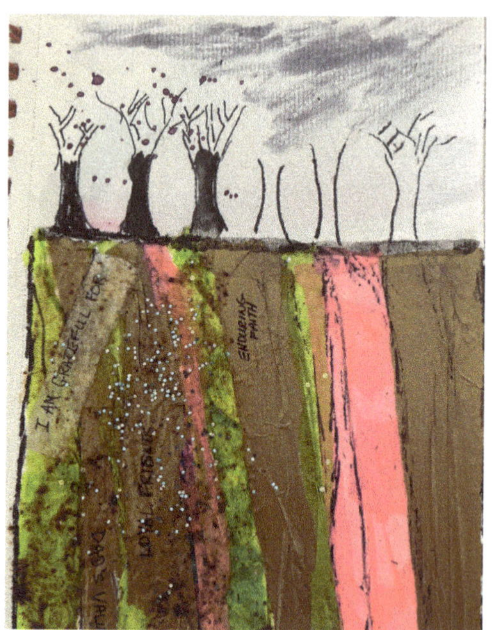

Above: Deep Roots, Unfinished Growth. Let our roots grow down in Him (Collos. 2:7). This watercolor is in response to the questions: What are the 'deep roots" in your life? What "fruits" are they bearing? God's people are like trees planted by water, bringing forth good fruit in their season (Psalm 1:3).

Left: Those leaves that once did, but that no longer serve the tree well - that are out of season now - let them fall away to the ground. As our country reflects on racism & injustice, let us all consider which of the leaves on our tree need to be shed and fall to the ground.

Lament: The Art of Mending
"Purposeful Stitching"
by Vivian Nix-Early
Mediums: water color, fabric, yarn, fern leaf, marker

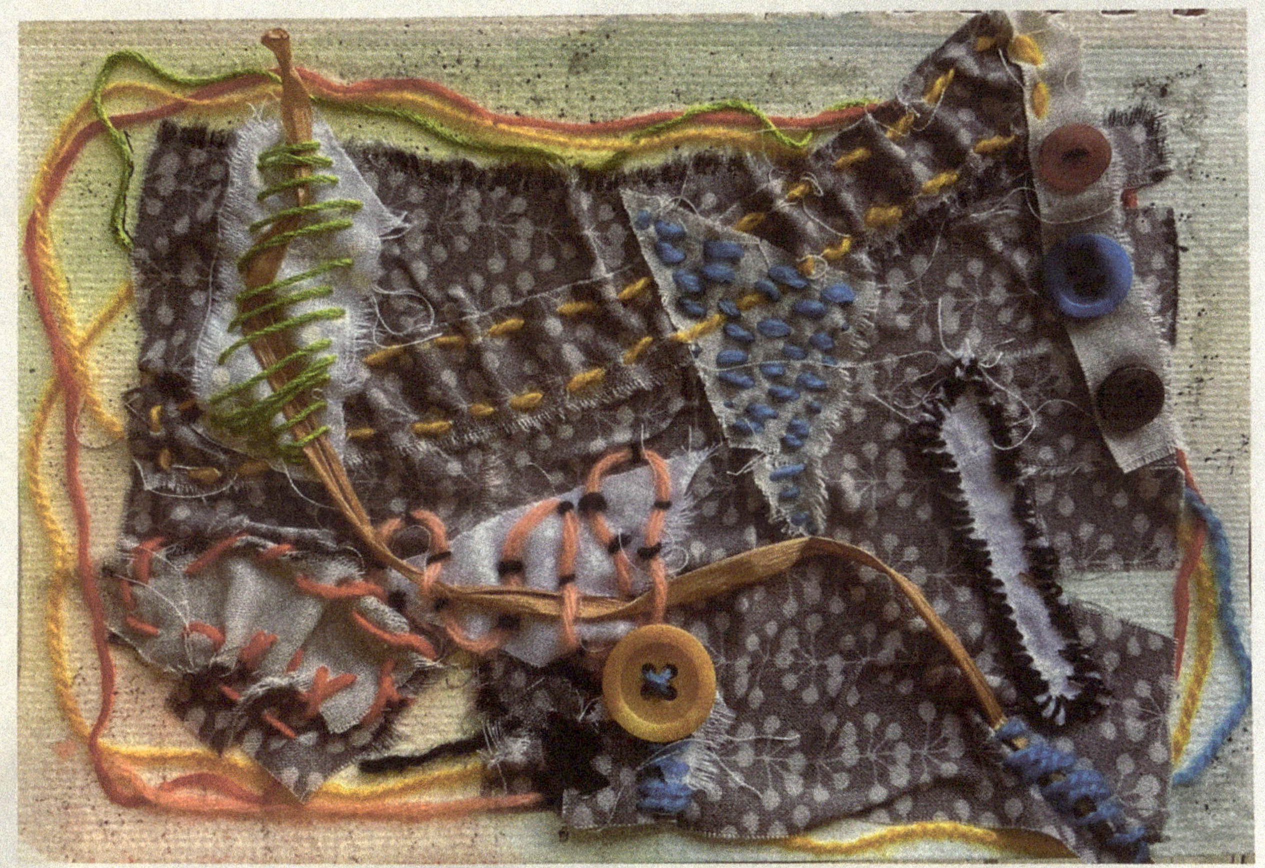

Just as each fabric piece ripped from the larger one takes on its own independent shape, so do each of life's wounds leave their unique scars and "spaces". The torn pieces in the artwork are purposefully overlapped, stitched, reinforced and reconnected in ways that preserve and maintain their visible uniqueness (or life "lesson"), while also becoming a new "whole" - stronger and more flexible. The almost dead fern leaf finds new life, meaning and purpose as a part of what binds, strengthens and heals. Finding ways to reconnect a torn spirit to God and His creation, can bring new strength, purpose and wholeness.

HOPE for the Country: The light shines in the
darkness, and the darkness has not overcome it.
(John 1:5)

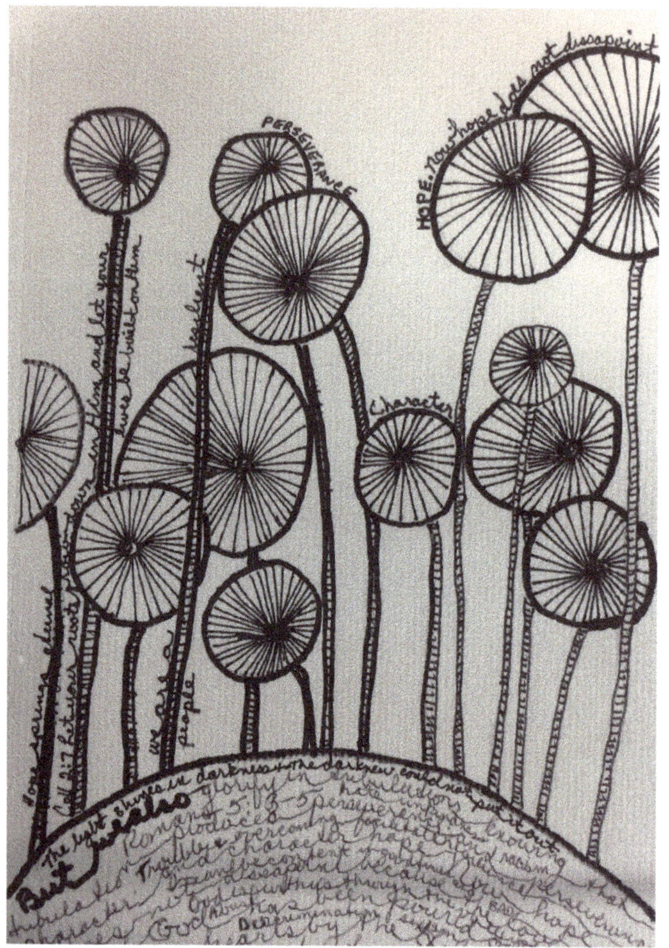

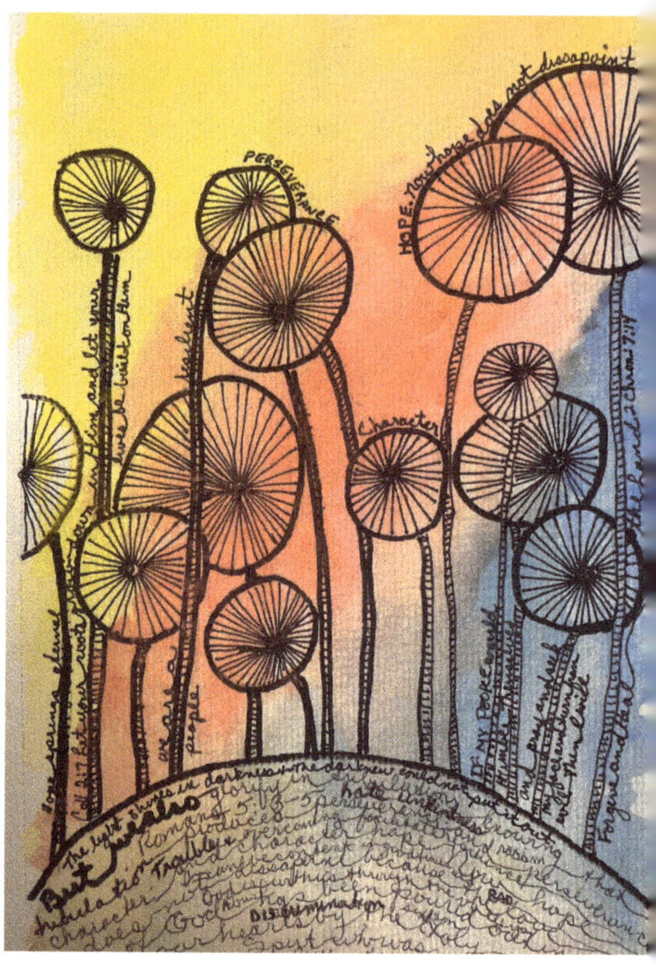

If my people who are called by my name humble
themselves, and pray and seek my face and turn
from their wicked ways, then I will hear from
heaven and will forgive their sin and heal their land.
(2 Chron. 7:14)

...we rejoice in our sufferings, knowing that suffering
produces endurance, and endurance produces
character, and character produces hope, and hope
does not put us to shame, because God's love has
been poured into our hearts through the Holy Spirit
who has been given to us. (Romans 5:3-5)

Art has been used as important social commentary for centuries.
Faith Ringgold is an "activist" artist who used the American flag in much of her work. In her style,
I offer this original "protest art" piece.

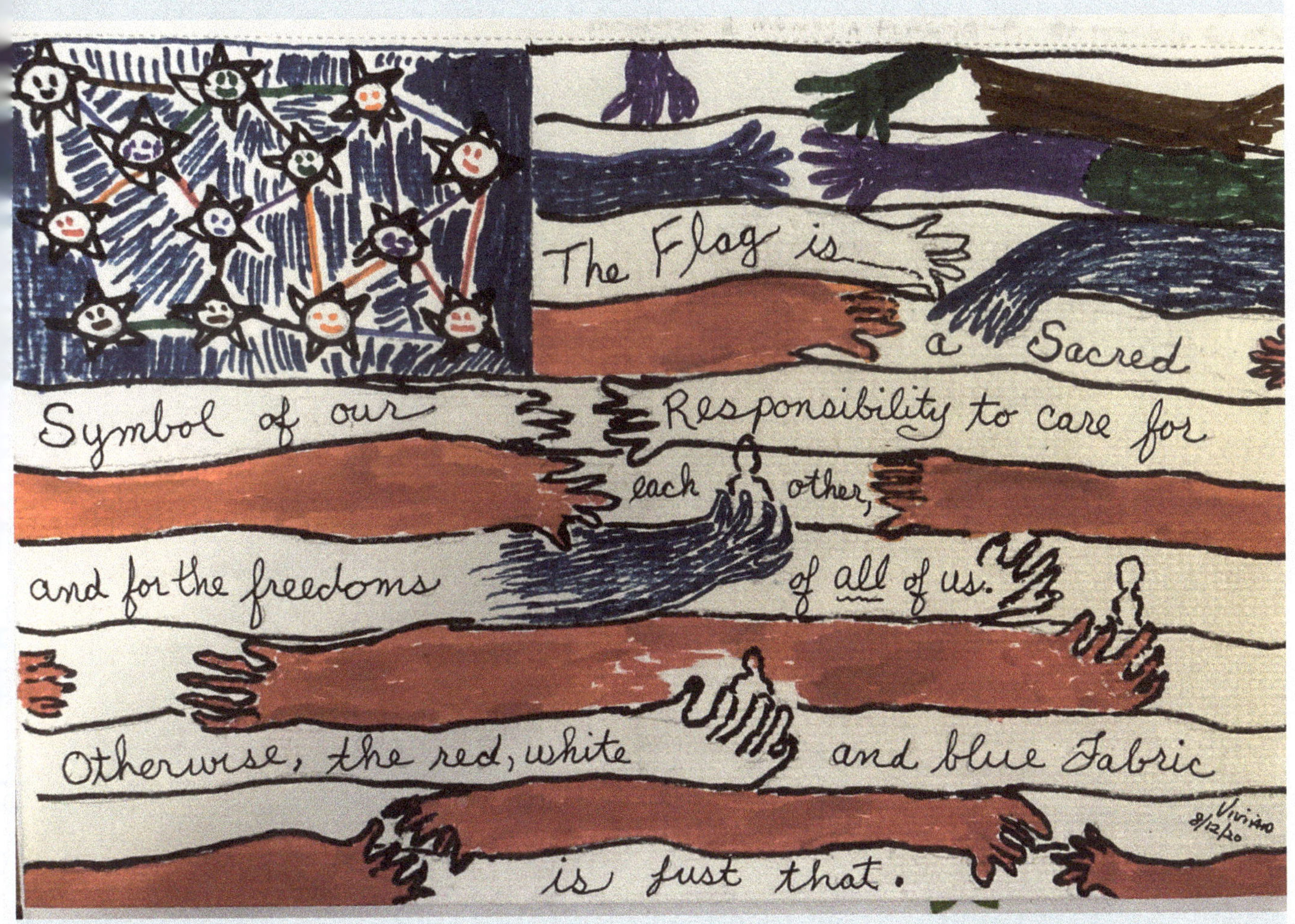

By July, the isolation was beginning to overwhelm me and I desperately needed to find a way to connect with other humans for a significant period of time. The virtual chats and weekly "Sunday at 6pm dancing in the street for 10 minutes" on my street and in our driveways had given some interpersonal relief, but not nearly with enough intimacy. Since COVID cases were very low in their area, I considered the possibility of a visit to my friends, especially since my 71st birthday was approaching.

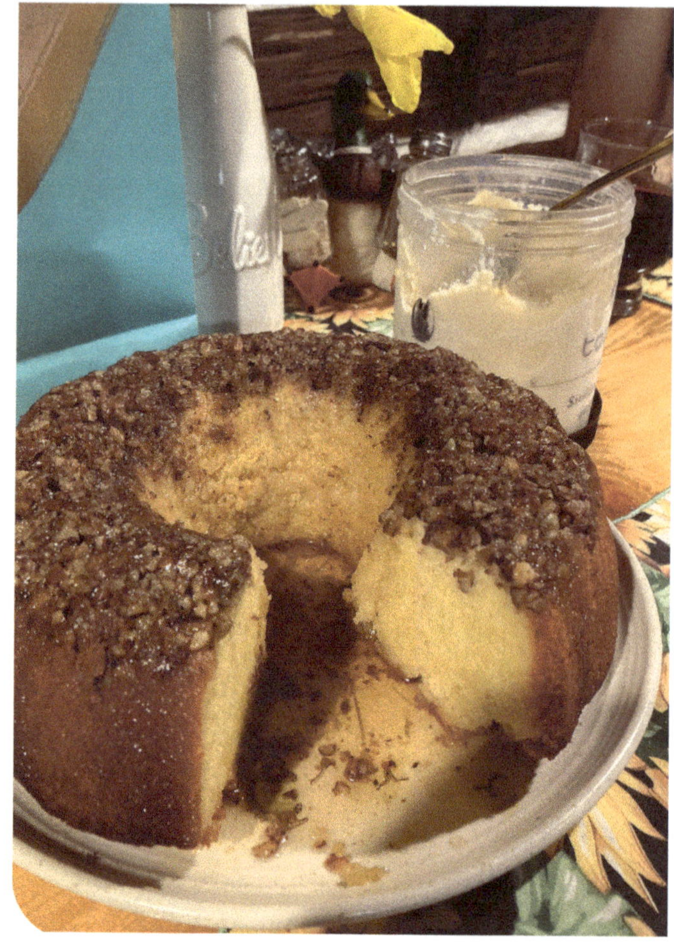

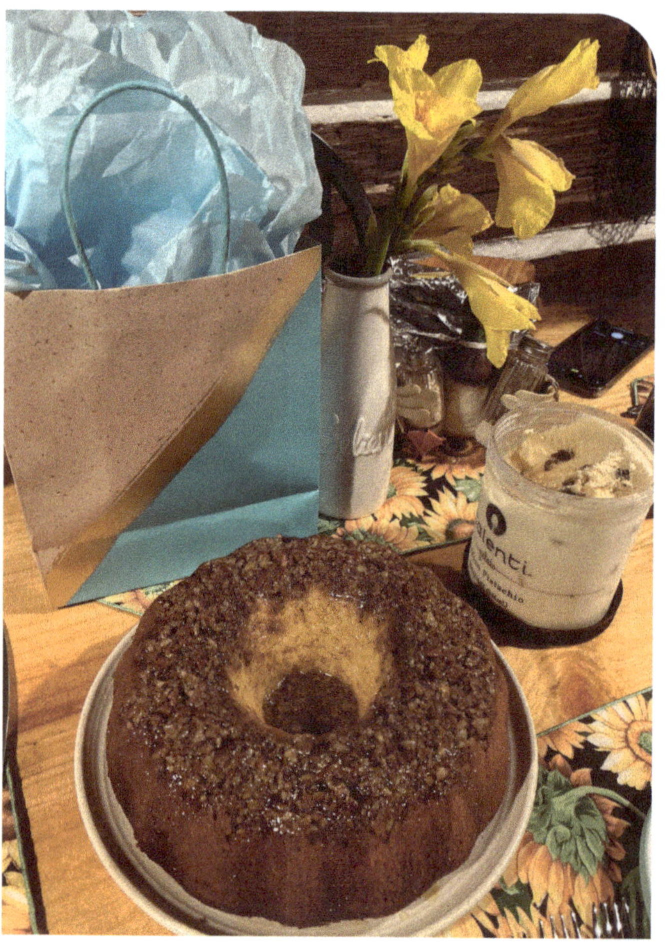

July 24th. I made this Key Lime Rum Cake, homemade rum raisin ice cream (above) and a Key Lime Crumb Cake (opp. page) as a birthday gift to myself. I packed it all up and shared it with my best friends, the Corbitts, at their rustic cabin in the North Carolina mountains. It was my first time being with other people since the beginning of the quarantine. I drove 6 hours to get there and made sure I got a COVID test before & after the visit. It was a restorative visit for us all.

These vegan triple-berry sheet pan pancakes seemed the ideal thing for a cabin breakfast.

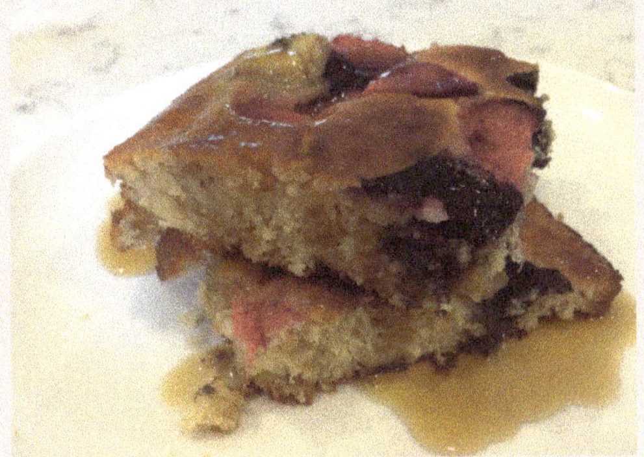

Self-care element: We create & maintain meaning for our lives by reconnecting with a higher power, nature, family, friends & virtual communities; or by volunteering and visiting places that have special meaning in order to feel grounded, hopeful and stable.

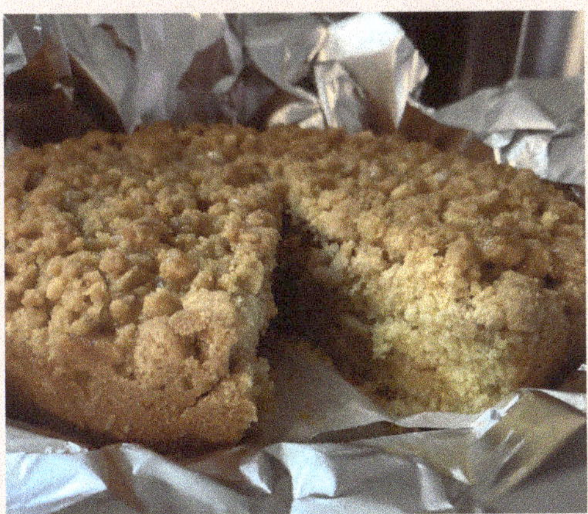

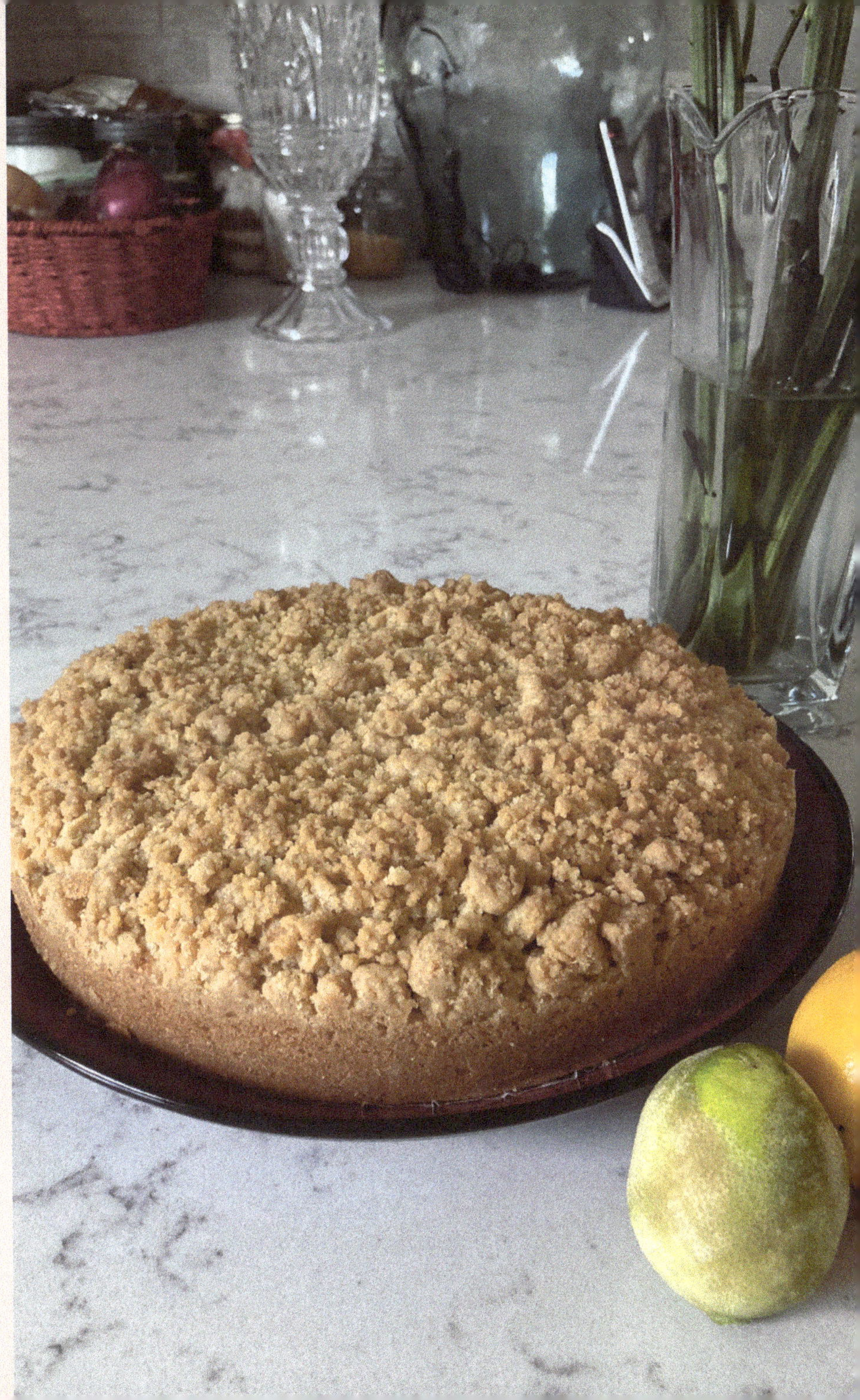

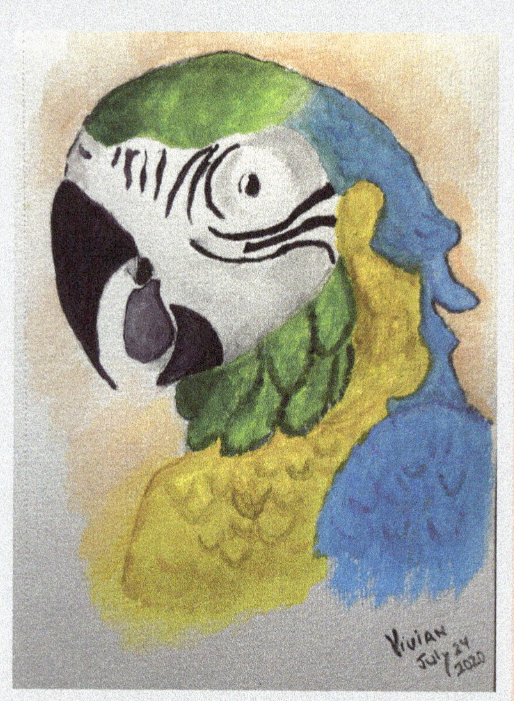

Vivian
July 24
2020

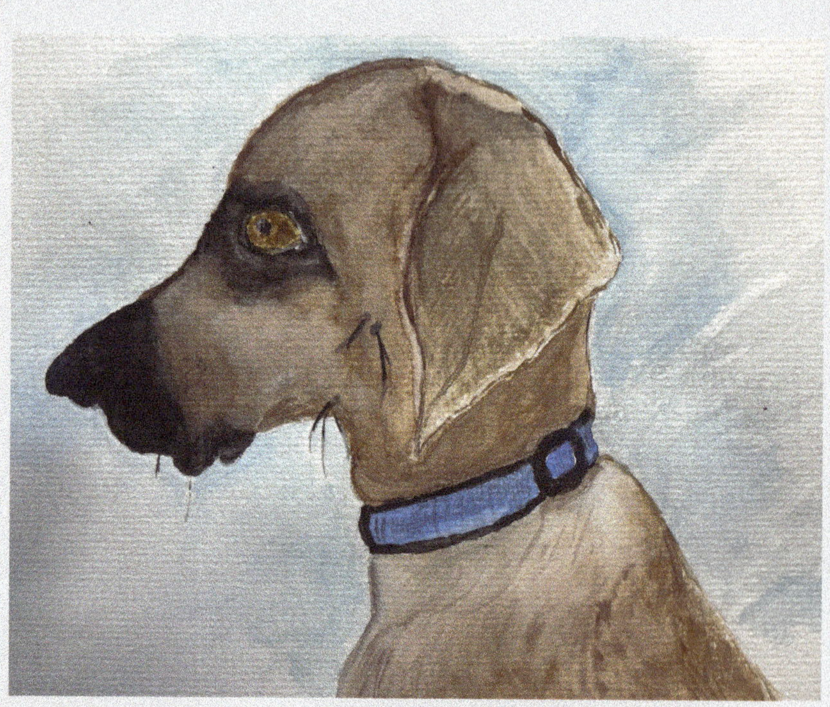

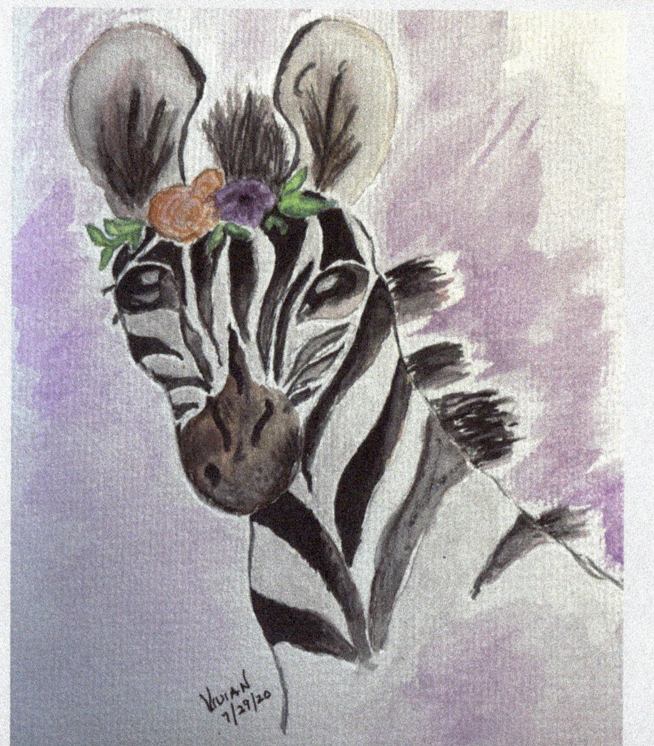

Vivian
7/29/20

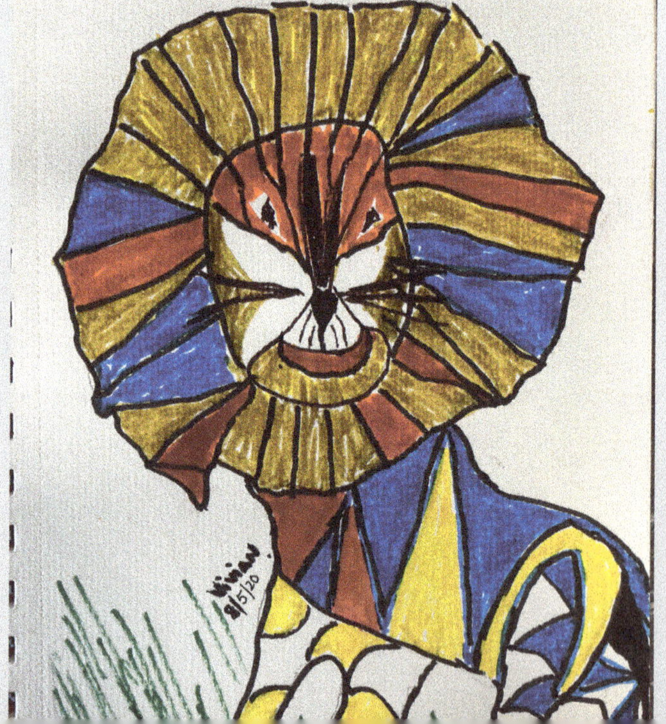

Vivian
8/5/20

Left: My loft in the North Carolina cabin was an ideal place to continue my online drawing classes. This class, through Athentikos, was how to sketch animals (parrot, zebra, dog). The dog is Zulu, the Corbitts' Ridgeback. The lion is drawn in the style of Picasso from a BuildaBridge online course on The Masters (that included Faith Ringgold and Alma Thomas).

Right: The cabin retreat also gave me time to begin this metaphoric tree that was my attempt to capture the basic message and theory from Ibram X. Kendi's book on How to Be an Antiracist. The symbolic nature of visual art is one of its communicative "powers". More on the tree at viviannixearly.life

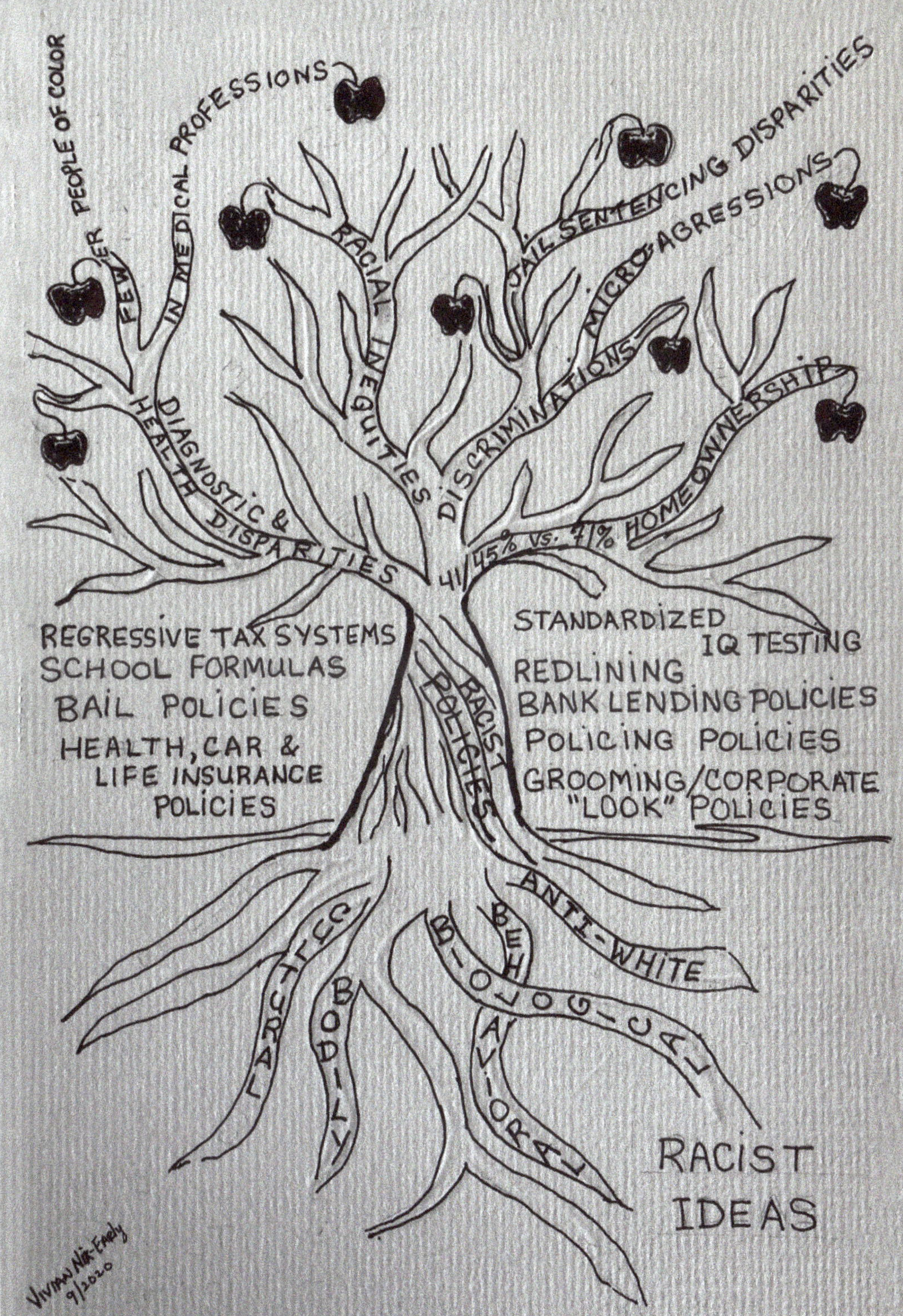

BREAD is a basic part of the diet for many cultures around the world. It holds symbolism in culture and literature as not only physical nourishment, but also spiritual nourishment. In faith practice, it symbolizes the ultimate gift from God, the giver of eternal life. It was often a focal point in Jesus' relationship with his followers, and breaking bread is an important part of our relationships now. The bread-making process has long been known to be therapeutic. As in clay therapy, the tactile nature of kneading the dough is a welcome antidote for anything from anxiety and tension to arthritic hands (which I am beginning to have!). Mindful breathing & prayer are healthy accompaniments that I employed while kneading. The process holds lessons in humility (simple ingredients), patience and delayed gratification as well as mystery & magic as the yeast bubbles to life in water; and as the rising process takes its good time.

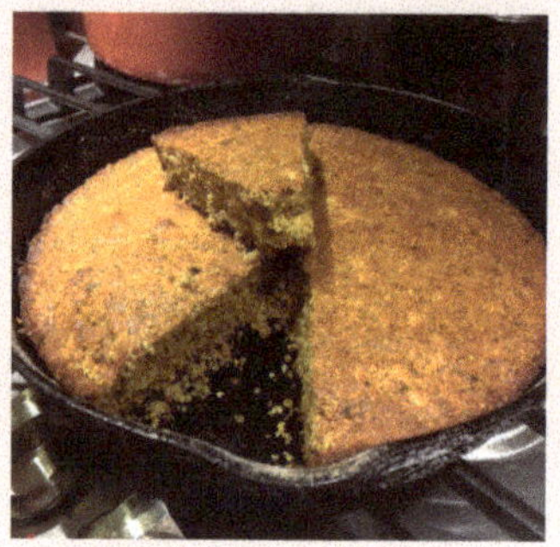

Cheddar Ranch Skillet Cornbread

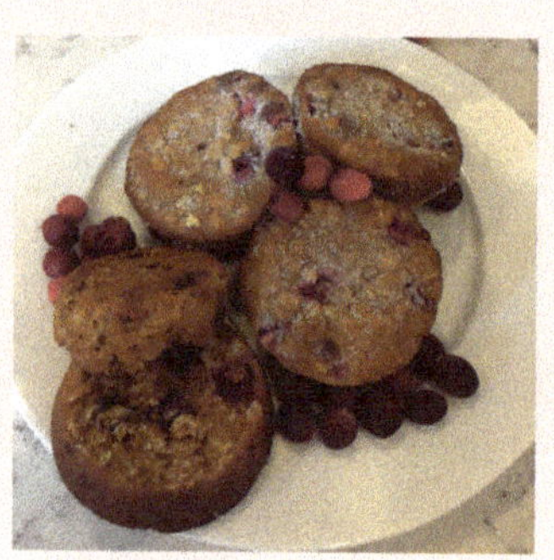

Cranberry Orange Muffins

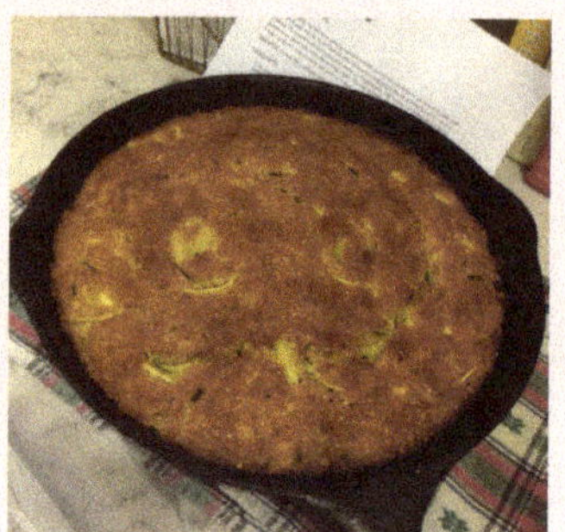

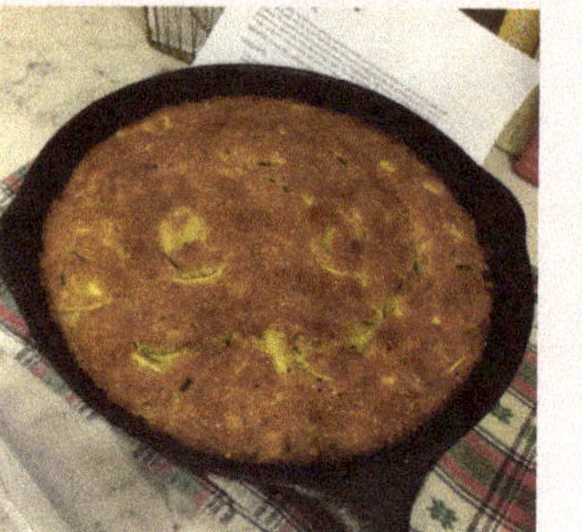

Zucchini Cornbread

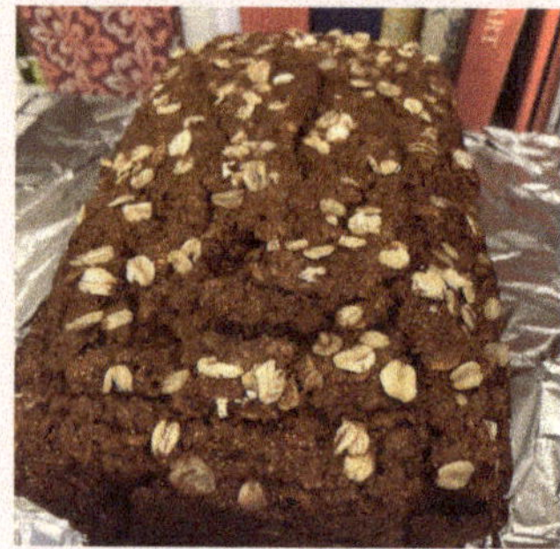

Oatmeal Banana Bread

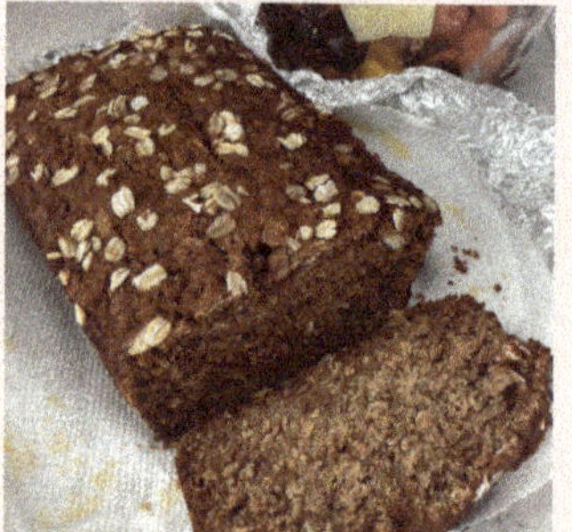

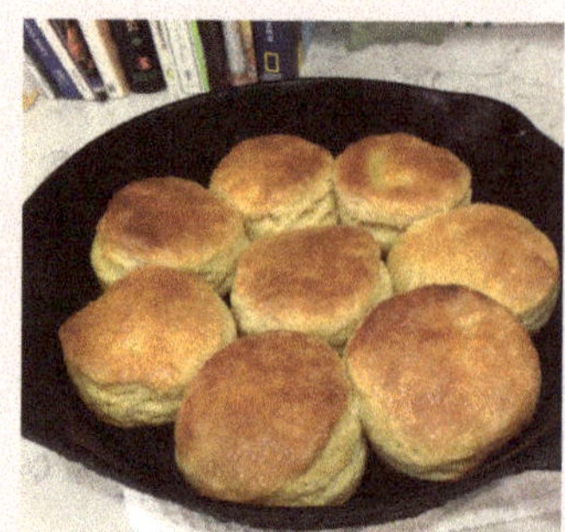

Chocolate Cherry Bread

Buttermilk Biscuits

For some recipes, I reached back to the time when I baked often. But most of these breads were new to my repertoire. It was fun experimenting with this life-giving staple, symbolic of hospitality & the absence of physical & spiritual hunger.

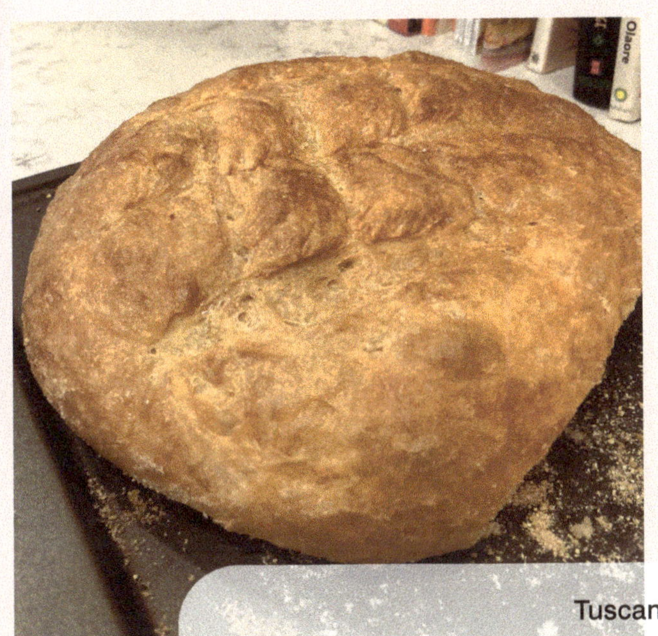

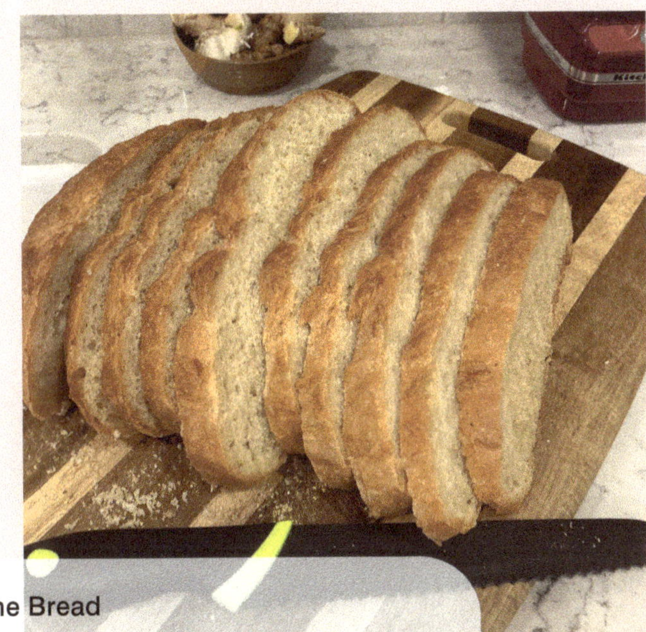

Tuscan Pane Bread

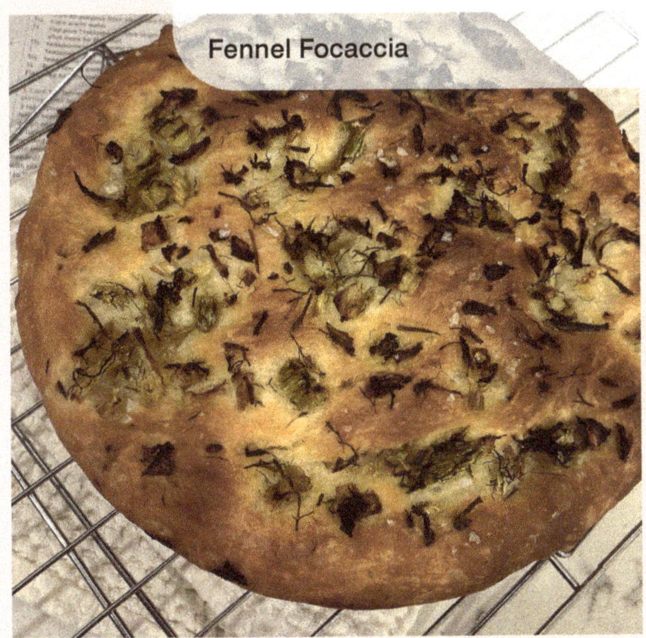

Fennel Focaccia

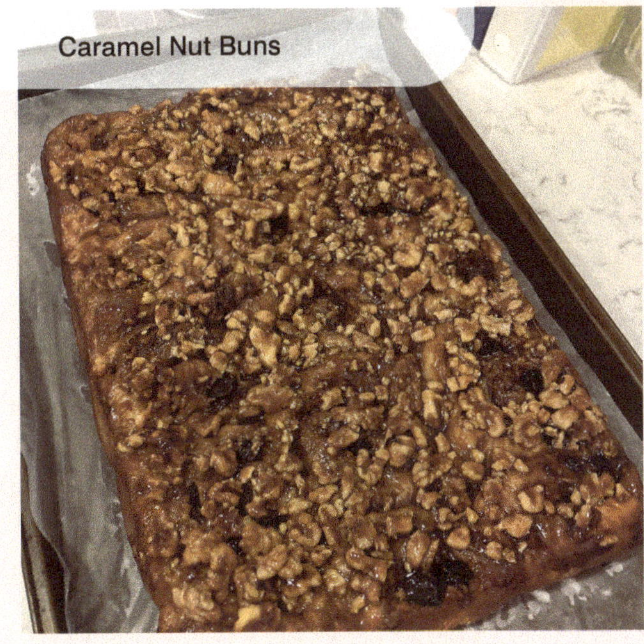

Caramel Nut Buns

The Blue Zones Kitchen book (available from Amazon) became my go-to bible for unusual plant-based recipes using root
vegetables and other world region ingredients that I'd never
heard of. Most of them were, surprisingly, available locally.
Dan Buettner, in conjunction with National Geographic,
identified the places around the world where people live the
longest (over 100).

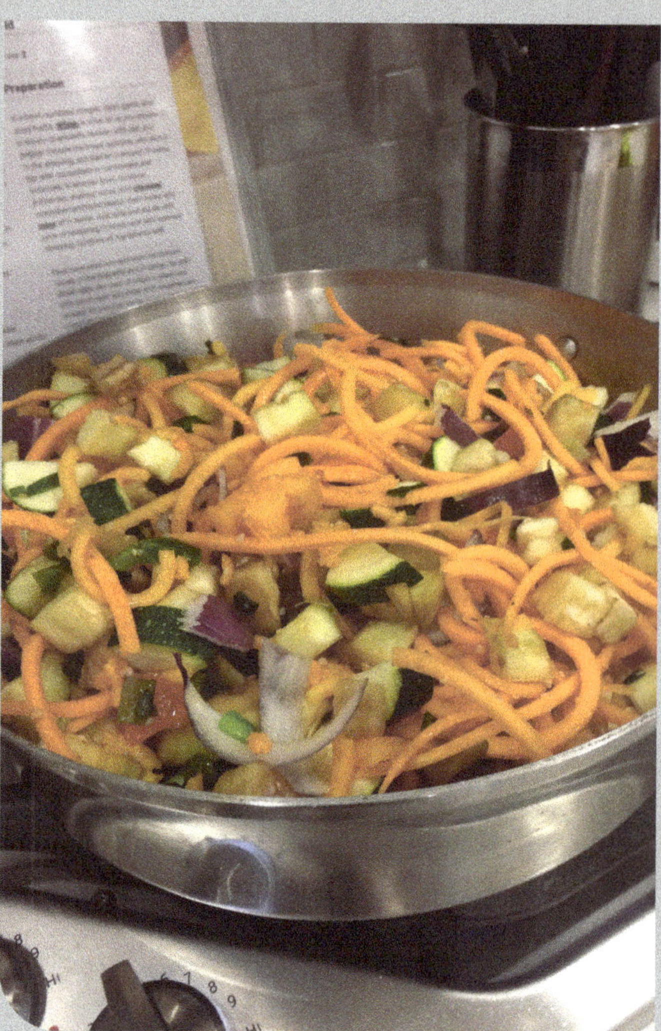

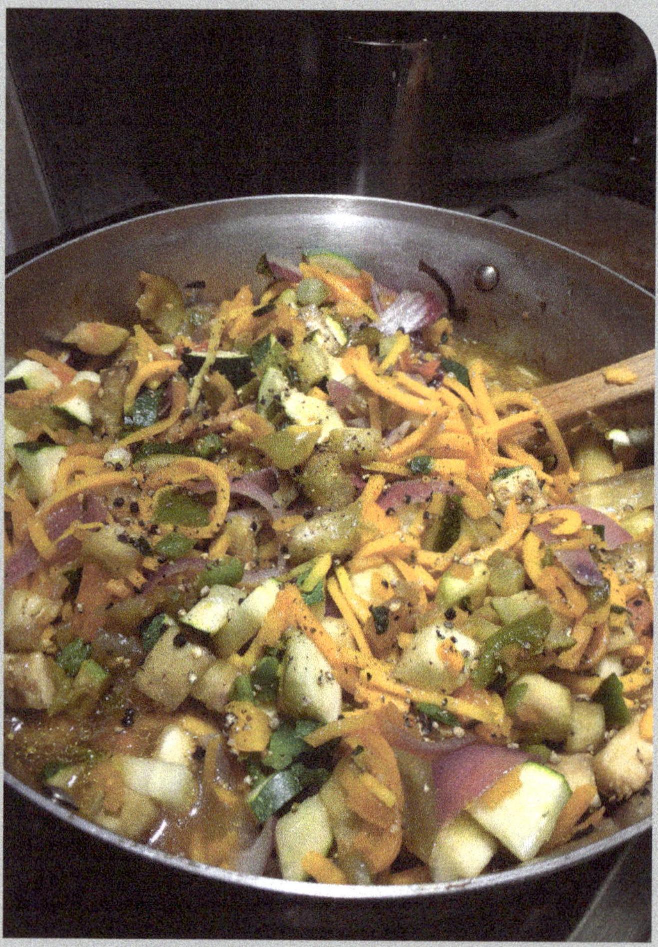

While diet was one of several life characteristics researched,
it was nevertheless a significant one that led to this book of
culture and food.

  Soft music or silence enhance mindful eating and breathing. Music is a soothing accompaniment to much of my crafting, cooking, sketching, journaling and praying. Music's powers include its ability to impart a sense of internal order through rhythm; and Involvement in music helps our brain secrete oxytocin that fosters social connection, decreases cortisol (the stress hormone), regulates our emotional responses, often giving a sense of calm, and promotes sleep.

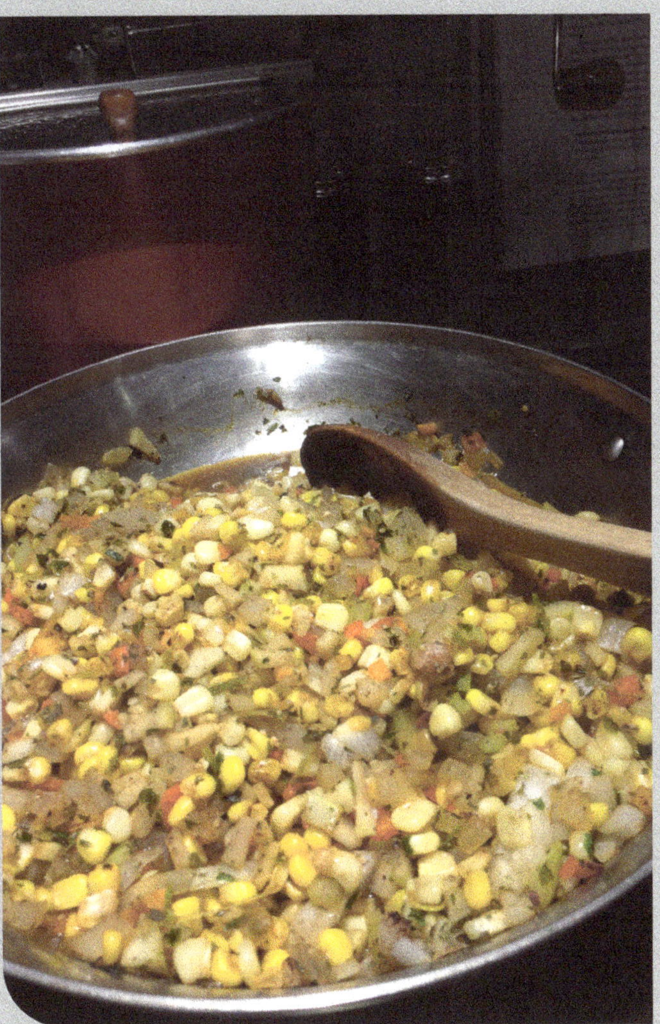

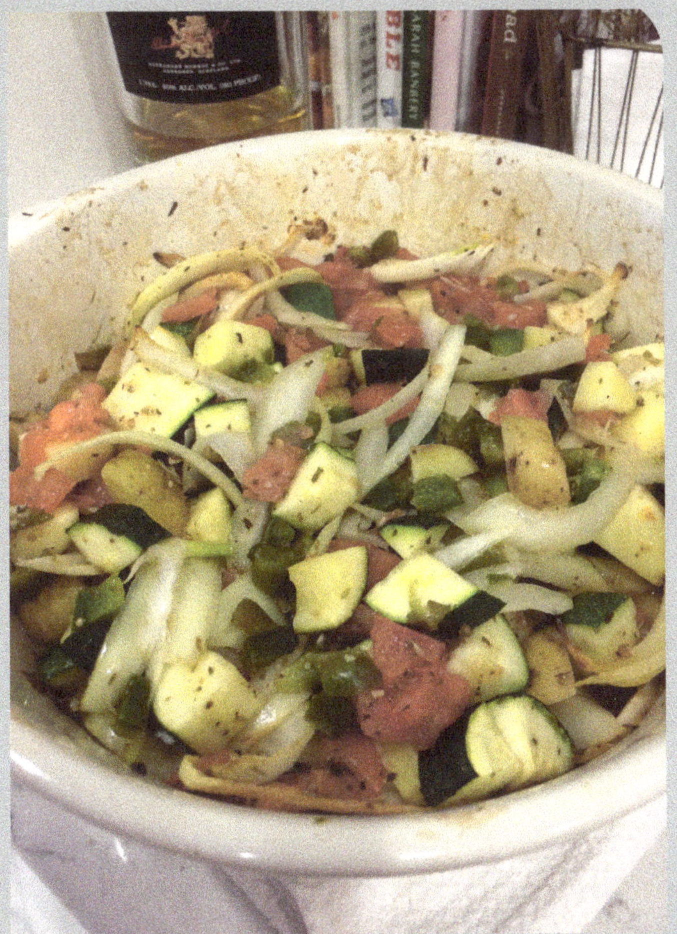

Some of my favorite music to accompany creating or for meditation & inspiration: The Pure Calm playlist from Apple Music Classical, updated every Thursday; Jon Batiste's jazz albums; music by Sheku Kanneh-Mason and the Kanneh-Mason family.

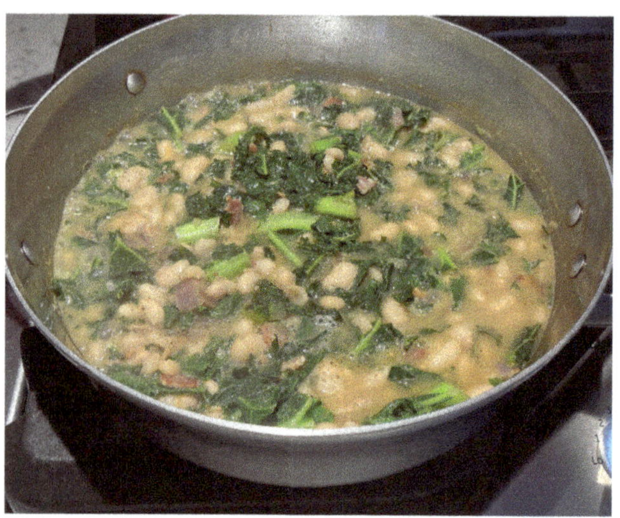

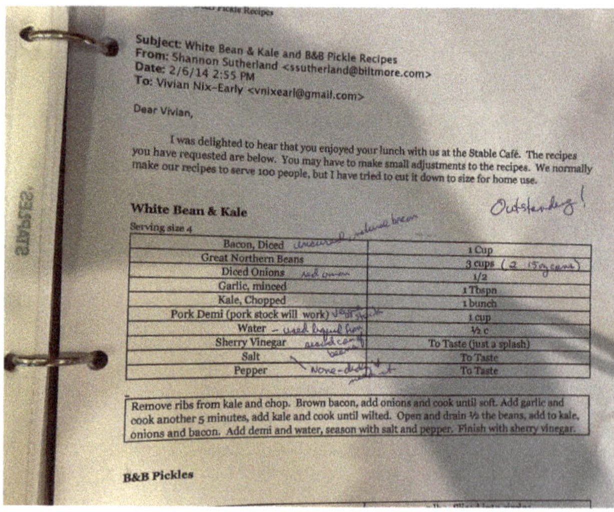

Pickle Recipes

Subject: White Bean & Kale and B&B Pickle Recipes
From: Shannon Sutherland <ssutherland@biltmore.com>
Date: 2/6/14 2:55 PM
To: Vivian Nix–Early <vnixearl@gmail.com>

Dear Vivian,

    I was delighted to hear that you enjoyed your lunch with us at the Stable Café. The recipes you have requested are below. You may have to make small adjustments to the recipes. We normally make our recipes to serve 100 people, but I have tried to cut it down to size for home use.

White Bean & Kale

Serving size 4

Bacon, Diced		1 Cup
Great Northern Beans		3 cups (2 15 oz cans)
Diced Onions		1/2
Garlic, minced		1 Tbspn
Kale, Chopped		1 bunch
Pork Demi (pork stock will work)		1 cup
Water		½ c
Sherry Vinegar		To Taste (just a splash)
Salt		To Taste
Pepper		To Taste

Remove ribs from kale and chop. Brown bacon, add onions and cook until soft. Add garlic and cook another 5 minutes, add kale and cook until wilted. Open and drain ½ the beans, add to kale, onions and bacon. Add demi and water, season with salt and pepper. Finish with sherry vinegar.

B&B Pickles

What goes better with a piece of freshly baked bread than a bowl of hearty, homemade soup. With the approach of the cooler winter months, soups became a passion in my pursuit of a more plant-based diet. This White Bean & Kale Soup and the Spicy Thai Sweet Potato Stew were two of my favorites.

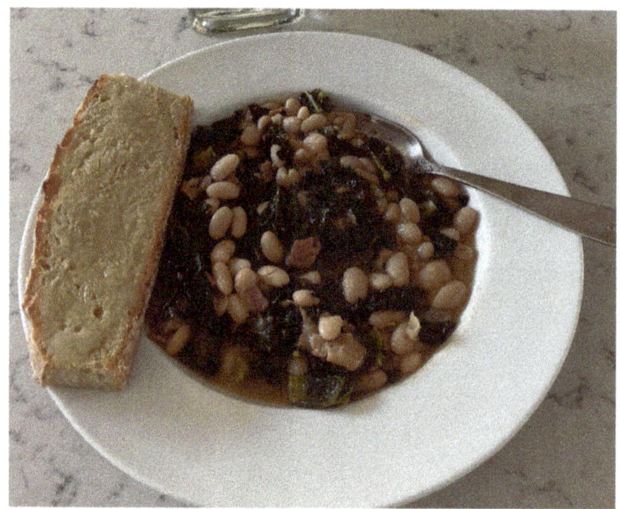

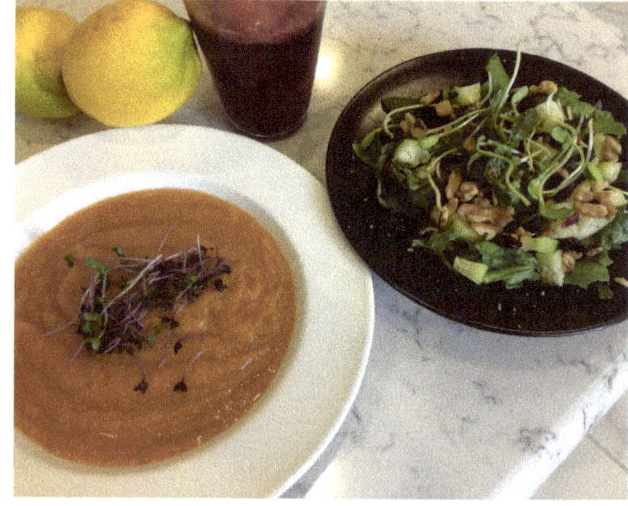

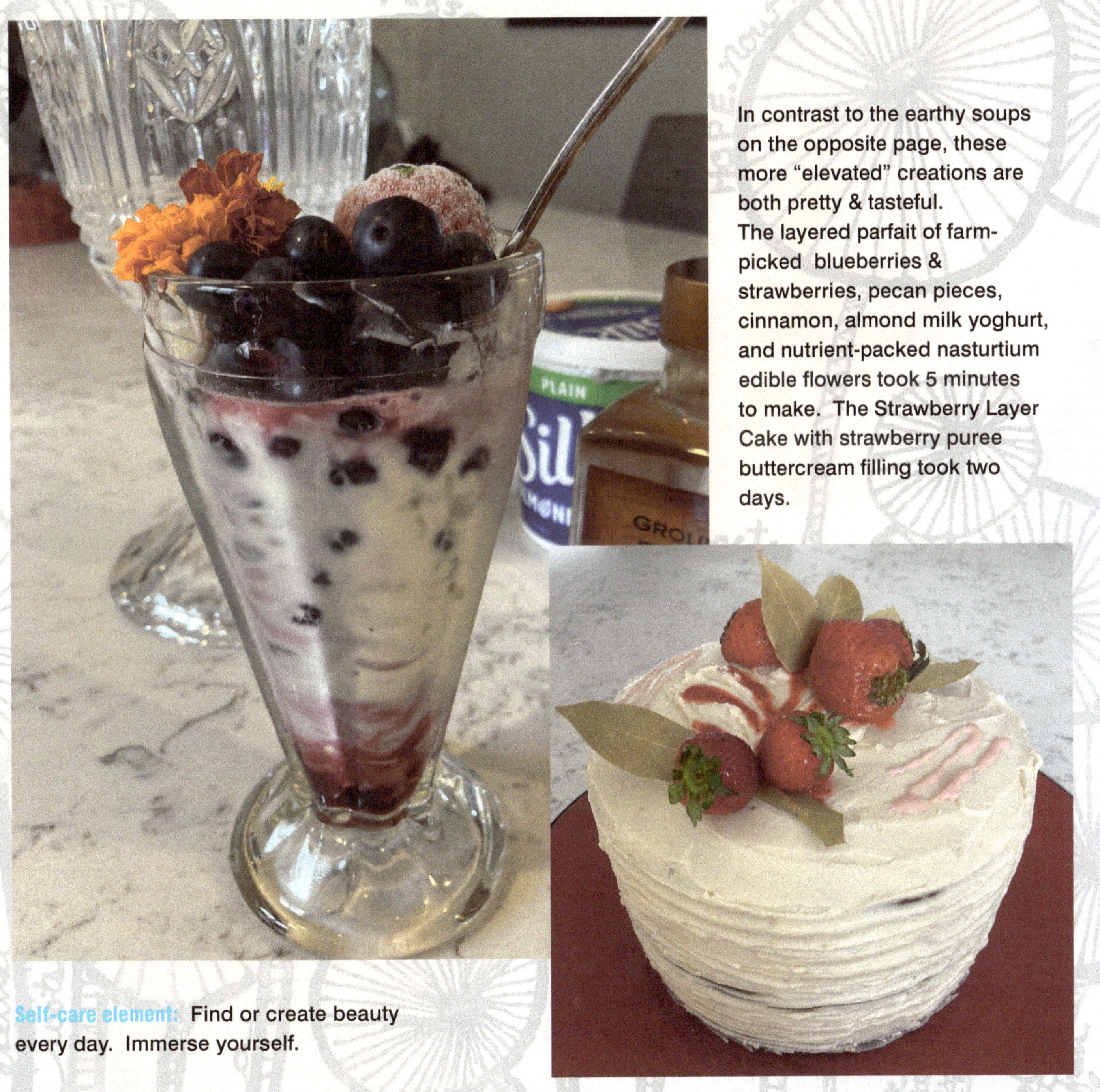

In contrast to the earthy soups on the opposite page, these more "elevated" creations are both pretty & tasteful.
The layered parfait of farm-picked blueberries & strawberries, pecan pieces, cinnamon, almond milk yoghurt, and nutrient-packed nasturtium edible flowers took 5 minutes to make. The Strawberry Layer Cake with strawberry puree buttercream filling took two days.

Self-care element: Find or create beauty every day. Immerse yourself.

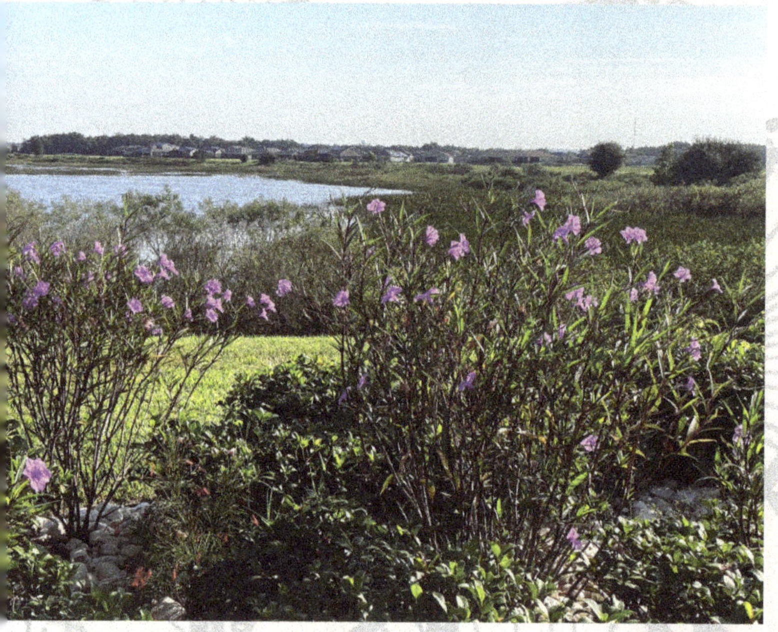

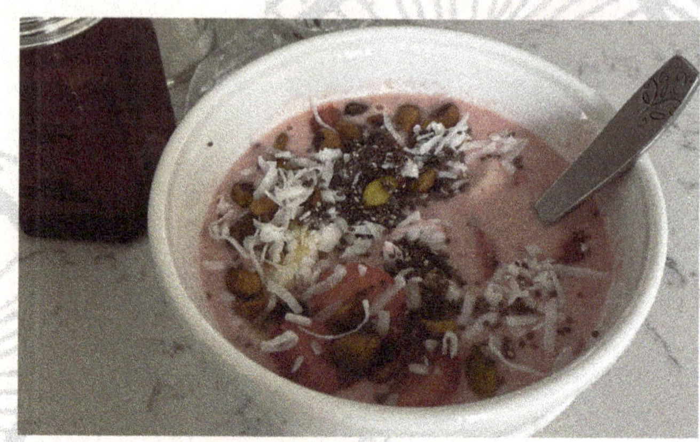

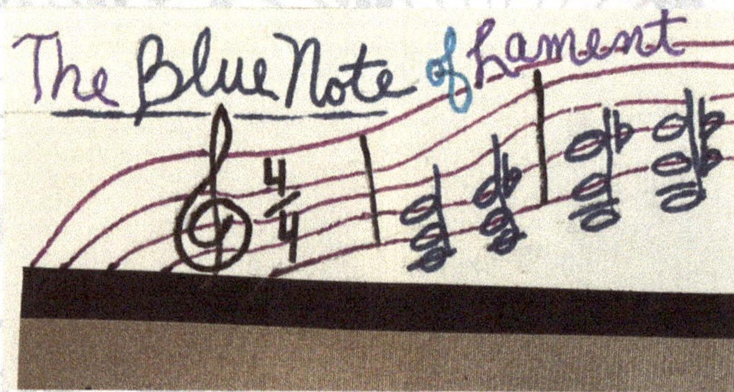

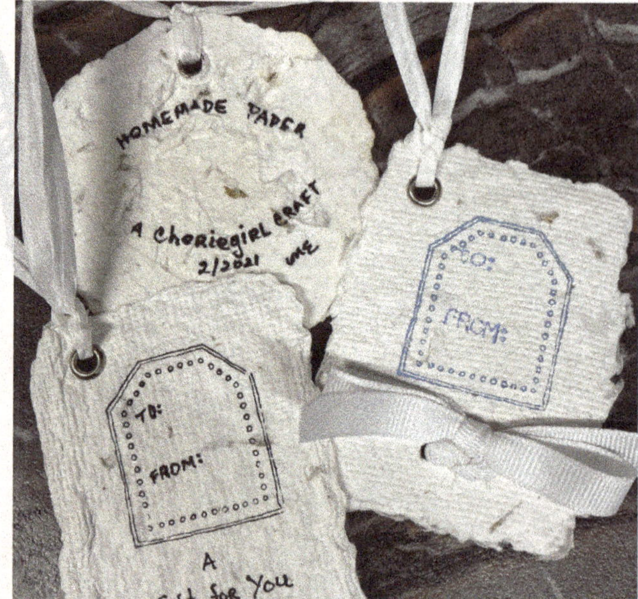

Experiencing a sense of beauty in our lives is one of a handful of universal needs that all humans possess. It is transcendent and as critical to our souls as bread and water is to our bodies. Probably like you, I find beauty in many things - music, nature, poetry, a giving heart, a face. I also found joy in creating & sharing the beauty in these culinary art pieces, homemade paper items, and a photograph I took of the view from my bedroom window turned into canvas wall art. There is also beauty in this chord progression I composed as a lament for the grief caused by the pandemic.

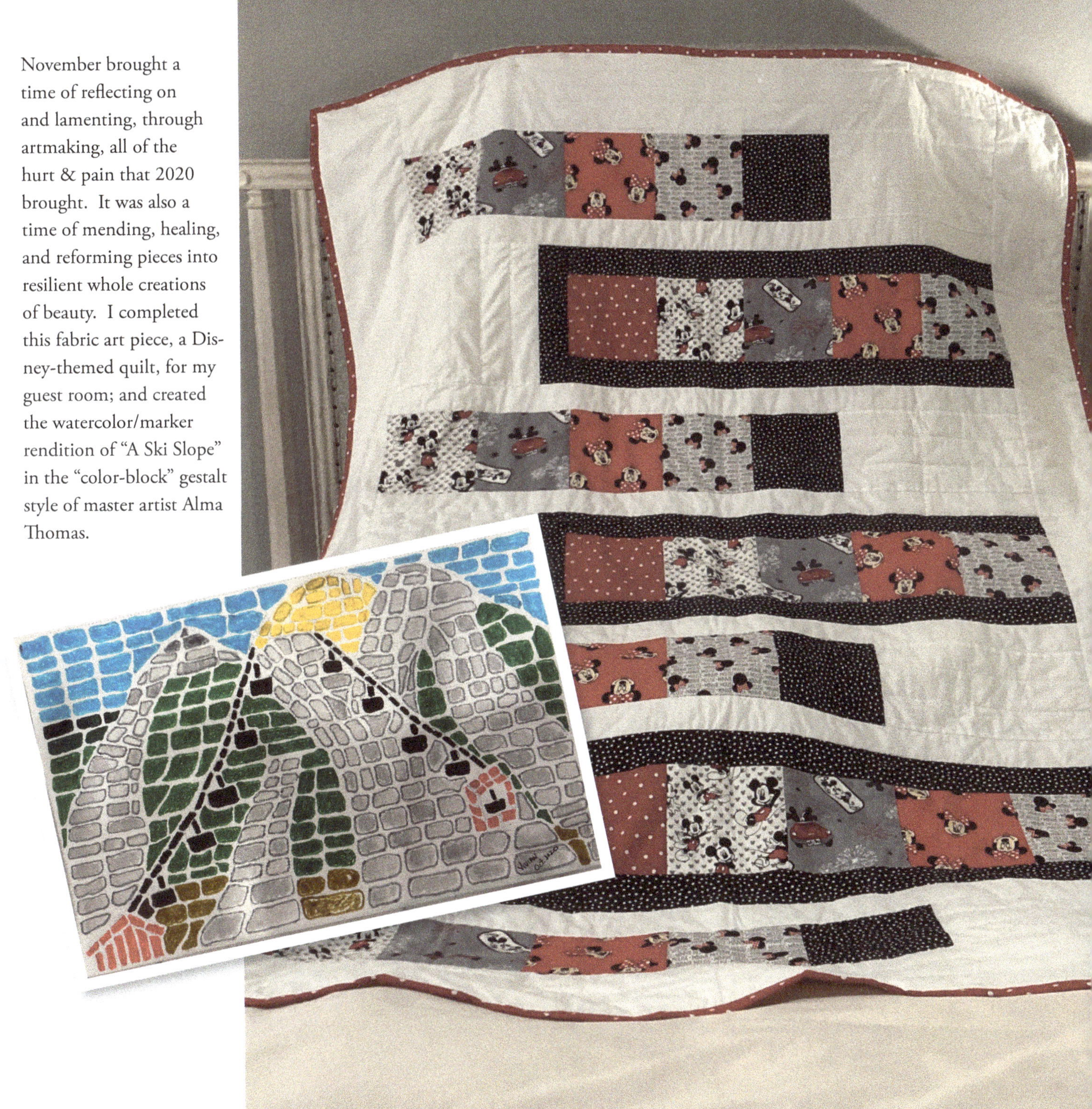

November brought a time of reflecting on and lamenting, through artmaking, all of the hurt & pain that 2020 brought. It was also a time of mending, healing, and reforming pieces into resilient whole creations of beauty. I completed this fabric art piece, a Disney-themed quilt, for my guest room; and created the watercolor/marker rendition of "A Ski Slope" in the "color-block" gestalt style of master artist Alma Thomas.

Swimming twice a week for an hour in the early morning in my community's heated outdoor pool became one of my self-care strategies. It was part of my Thursday & Sunday morning ritual. Having just shed the stress of serving as a volunteer for the presidential election, I created this pressed flower poetry piece to capture the "new, life-giving" experience of immersion into the water, receiving God's peace in nature.

Self-care elements:

 First, regular exercise and activities that maintain physical fitness, strength and aerobic conditioning are a must.

Second, intentional, daily rituals are one of the most important self-care strategies, especially amidst seeming chaos. They facilitate a sense of internal order & calm, keep us grounded, feeling in control, and experiencing the world as more predictable. My early morning ritual includes exercise followed by a superfoods smoothie, meditation/prayer and mindful breathing, often with soft music as an accompaniment. My evening ritual includes some expression (journal, mantra, drawing) of gratitude.

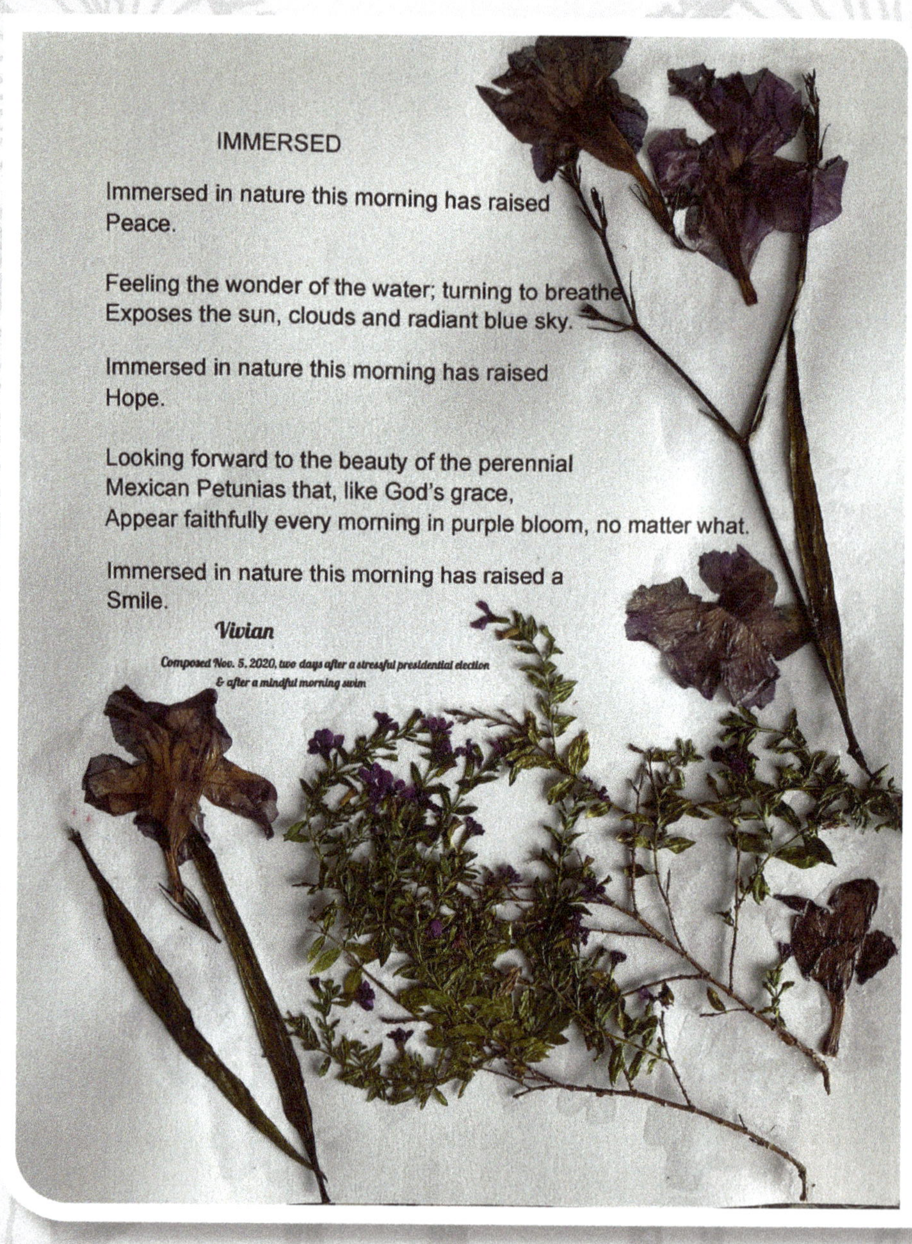

IMMERSED

Immersed in nature this morning has raised
Peace.

Feeling the wonder of the water; turning to breathe
Exposes the sun, clouds and radiant blue sky.

Immersed in nature this morning has raised
Hope.

Looking forward to the beauty of the perennial
Mexican Petunias that, like God's grace,
Appear faithfully every morning in purple bloom, no matter what.

Immersed in nature this morning has raised a
Smile.

Vivian

Composed Nov. 5, 2020, two days after a stressful presidential election
& after a mindful morning swim

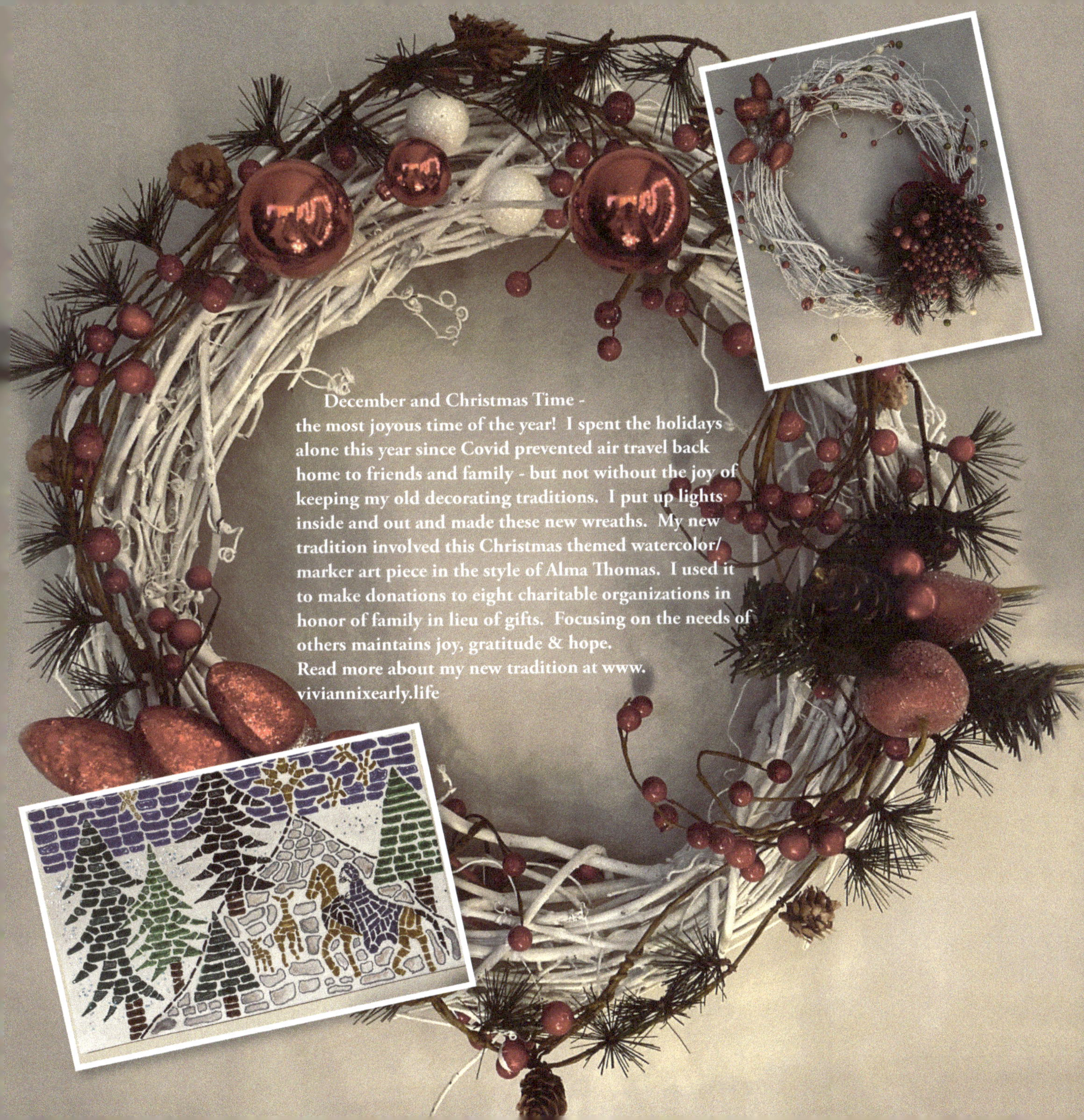

December and Christmas Time -
the most joyous time of the year! I spent the holidays
alone this year since Covid prevented air travel back
home to friends and family - but not without the joy of
keeping my old decorating traditions. I put up lights
inside and out and made these new wreaths. My new
tradition involved this Christmas themed watercolor/
marker art piece in the style of Alma Thomas. I used it
to make donations to eight charitable organizations in
honor of family in lieu of gifts. Focusing on the needs of
others maintains joy, gratitude & hope.
Read more about my new tradition at www.
viviannixearly.life

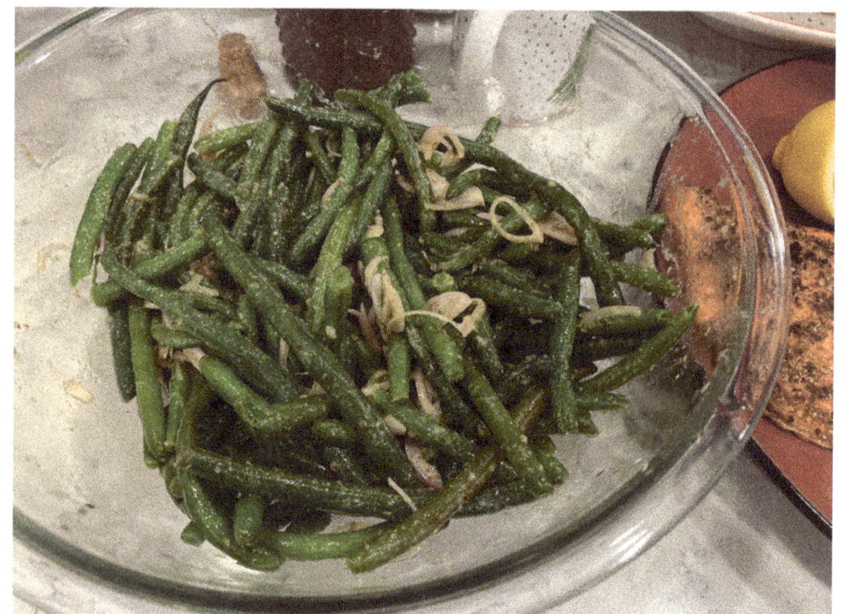

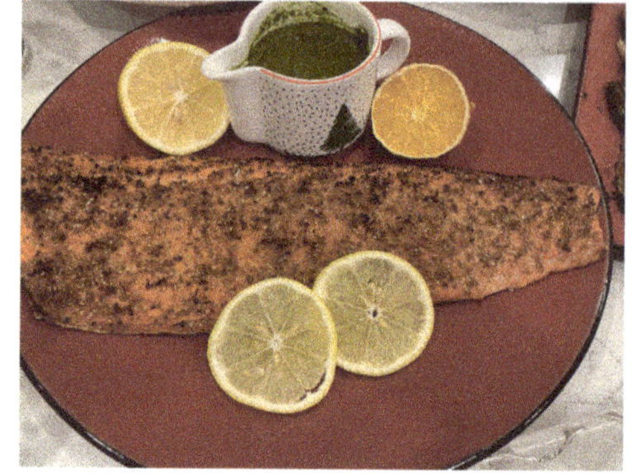

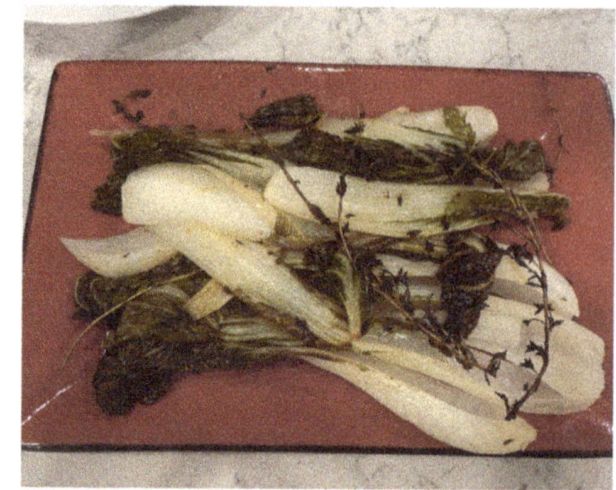

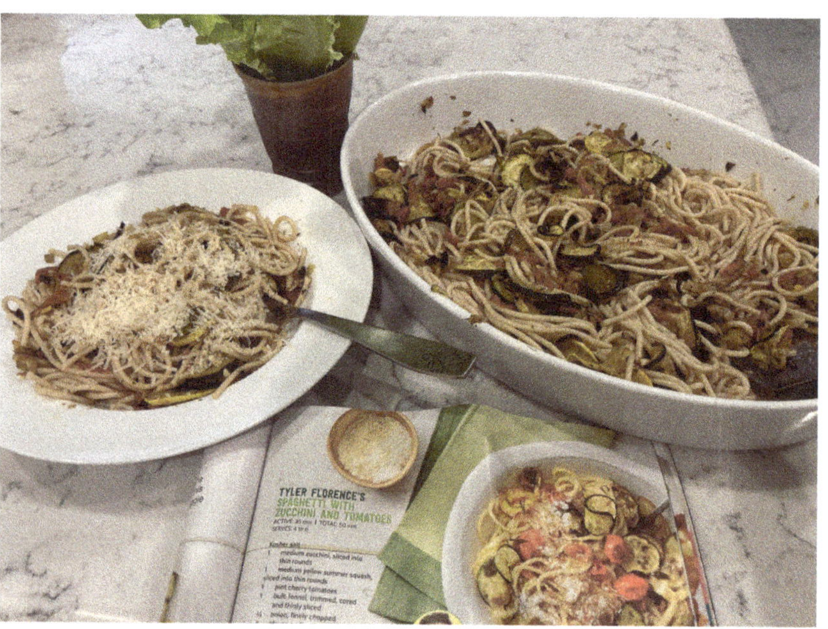

Christmas has always meant good food, and lots of it. This year, I was only cooking for me (and the freezer). But I wanted to create the "big meal" feeling we always have when everyone gathers together. Planning the unusual menu (I moved away from the standard Christmas dinner years ago) took most of November and December and served as restorative play time for my soul.

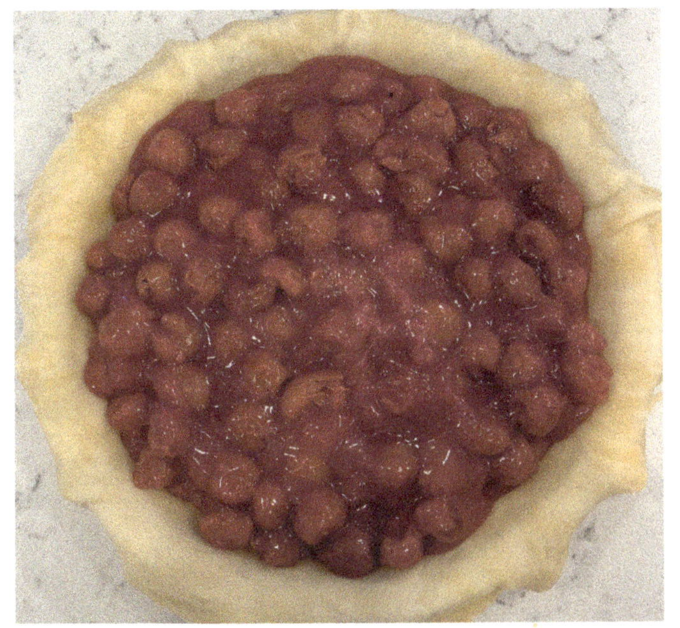

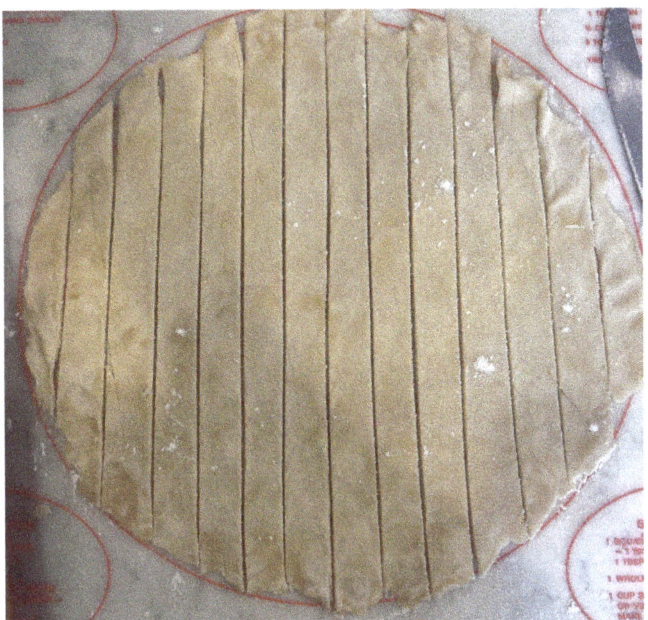

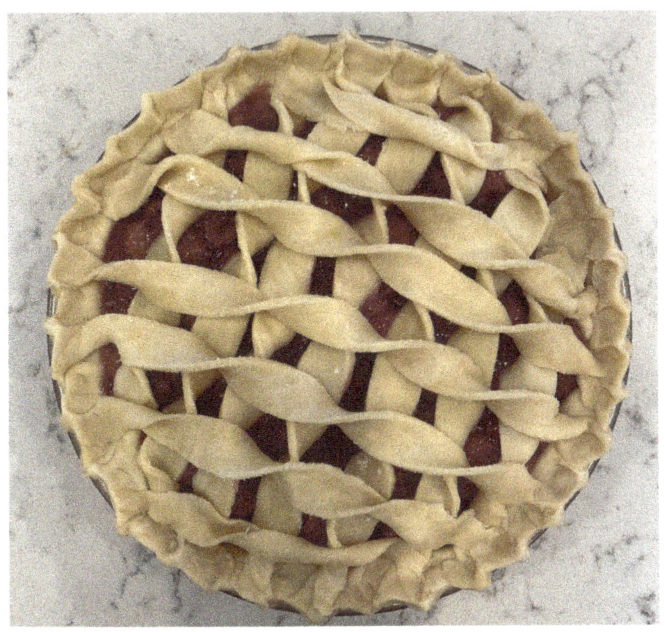

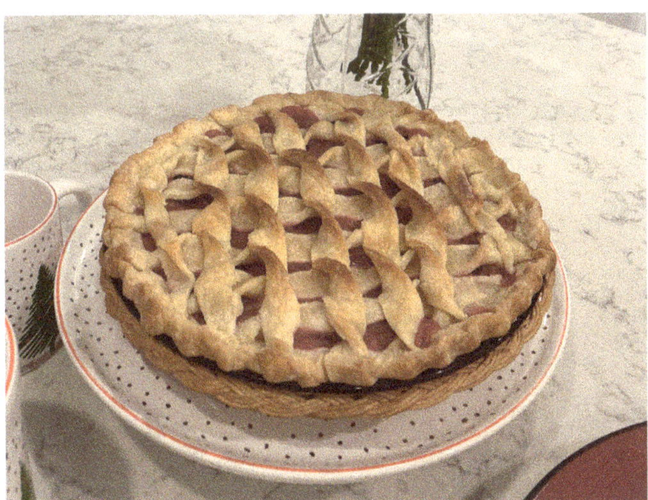

I immediately settled on the dessert, my favorite of all time: Sour Cherry Pie. I hadn't made it in years and was looking forward to revisiting an old recipe.

THE FINAL MENU

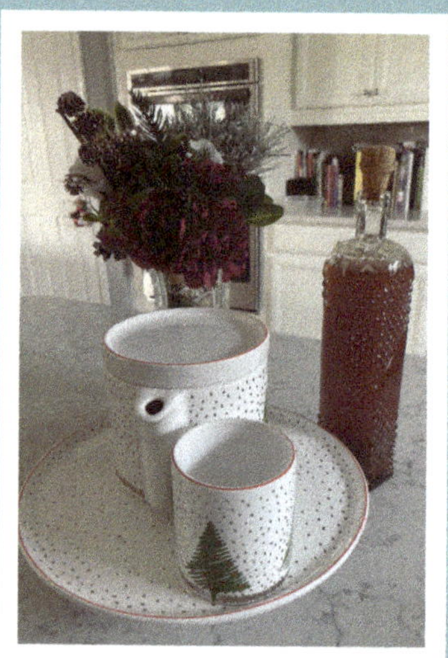 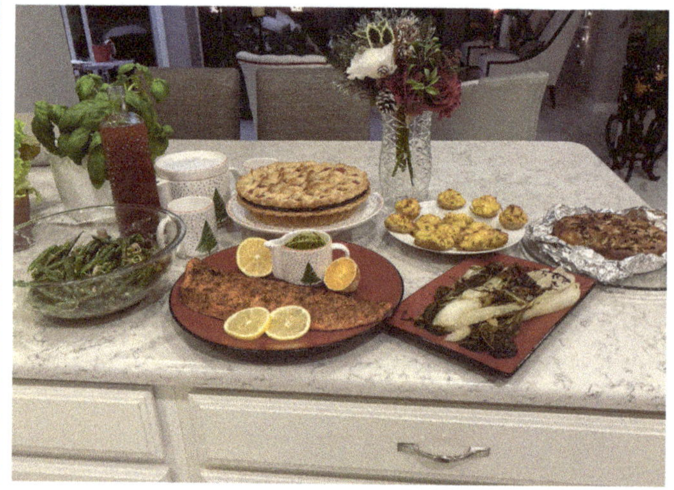

Spice-Rubbed Salmon with Herb Sauce; Spaghetti with Zucchini and Tomatoes; Lemon Rice; Green Beans with Mustard Vinaigrette; Twice-Baked Cheddar Mini Potatoes; Baby Bok Choy with Thyme; Cranberry Brie Wreath; Sour Cherry Pie; Fennel Focaccia Bread; Cranberry-Orange Cider.

Christmas day was spent eating and face-timing & texting with family & friends. I can see God's hand moving & working all things together for the good of those who love Him and who are called to His plan. (Romans 8:28) The year is ending with hope.